The Resurrection of Jesus Christ

The Resurrection of
Jesus Christ

by
John MacArthur, Jr.

MOODY PRESS
CHICAGO

All Scripture quotations, unless noted otherwise, are from the *New Scofield
Reference Bible*, King James Version. Copyright © 1967 by Oxford University Press, Inc. Reprinted by permission.

ISBN: 0-8024-5376-7

1 2 3 4 5 6 7 8 Printing/LC/Year 94 93 92 91 90 89

Printed in the United States of America

Contents

These Bible studies are taken from messages delivered by Pastor-Teacher John MacArthur, Jr., at Grace Community Church in Panorama City, California. The recorded messages themselves may be purchased as a series or individually. Please request the current price list by writing to:

WORD OF GRACE COMMUNICATIONS
P.O. Box 4000
Panorama City, CA 91412

Or call the following toll-free number:
1-800-55-GRACE

1
The Amazing Burial of Jesus Christ
—Part 1

Outline

Introduction

Lesson
I. Joseph of Arimathea (vv. 57-60)
   A. God's Timing (v. 57a)
      1. The preparation
         a) Its importance
         b) Its implications
            (1) No body could remain on a cross
            (2) Death needed to be hastened
      2. The prophecies
         a) Christ's unbroken legs
         b) Christ's pierced side
   B. God's Man (vv. 57b-60)
      1. His identification (v. 57b-c)
         a) As a rich man (v. 57b)
            (1) His characteristics
            (2) His home
         b) As a disciple of Christ (v. 57c)
      2. His commitment (v. 58)
         a) A high price
         b) A deep love
      3. His actions (vv. 59-60)
         a) He carried the body (v. 59a)
         b) He wrapped it in linen (v. 59b)
         c) He laid it in the tomb (v. 60a)
         d) He rolled a stone in front of the tomb (v. 60b)

II. The Two Marys (v. 61)
   A. Their Description (v. 61*a*)
   B. Their Significance (v. 61*b*)
      1. They saw the evidence
      2. They were commanded to give testimony
      3. They met the resurrected Christ

Introduction

Matthew 27:57-65 is a text of Scripture often passed over rapidly. Many of us aren't familiar with it. It does not contain any particularly memorable verses. It appears to be a routine portion of Scripture that discusses the burial of Jesus Christ. But in actuality it teaches us astounding truth.

Anyone knowledgeable about the Christian faith is aware of the significance of the cross, where our sins were borne by the Lord Jesus Christ to free us from the penalty and guilt of sin. Just as significant is the resurrection of Jesus Christ—the single greatest miracle the world will ever know. It demonstrates Christ's finished work of redemption and reminds us that His power over death will bring us to glory.

Between the crucifixion and resurrection of Christ is His burial. It's a marvelous account of God's intervention into every detail in the life of Christ. We see God's testimony unfold through Joseph of Arimathea (vv. 57-60), the two Marys (v. 61), and the chief priests and Pharisees (vv. 62-66). They play important roles in the burial of Jesus, validating the truthfulness of Christ's claim to be the Son of God.

Lesson

I. JOSEPH OF ARIMATHEA (vv. 57-60)

Two Key Prophecies

Two explicit prophecies had to be fulfilled in the burial of Jesus.

1. Isaiah 53:9

   The entire chapter of Isaiah 53 is devoted to the death of Christ. It says Christ was despised and rejected, truly a man of sorrows (v. 3). He bore our griefs and carried our sorrows (v. 4). He was wounded for our transgressions and bruised for our iniquities (v. 5). He was taken from prison into judgment (v. 8). Verse 9 says, "His grave was assigned to be with wicked men, yet He was with a rich man in His death" (NASB*). That unusual prophecy would be difficult to understand apart from the scenario of Christ's burial. He was supposed to have been buried with criminals, but instead He was buried in a rich man's tomb.

2. Matthew 12:40

   Jesus said, "Just as Jonah was three days and three nights in the belly of the sea monster, so shall the Son of Man be three days and three nights in the heart of the earth" (NASB). Jesus predicted that there would be three days between His death and resurrection—that He would be in the earth for three days.

The two prophecies just mentioned clearly refer to the burial of Christ. God used Joseph of Arimathea to fulfill those prophecies and thus provide testimony to the deity of Christ.

   A. God's Timing (v. 57*a*)

   "When the evening was come."

   The "evening" referred to is the early evening of the Jewish day (from 3:00 P.M. to 6:00 P.M.). The Sabbath began at 6:00 P.M. and ended at 6:00 P.M. the next day. So the setting of verse 57 is around 3:00 P.M. Jesus was nailed on the cross at 9:00 A.M., but by 3:00 P.M. He had died. That fact in itself is amazing—most victims lingered on the cross much longer, some for several days. No one took Christ's life from Him;

New American Standard Bible.

9

He voluntarily gave it up (John 10:17-18). Pontius Pilate, the Roman governor who ordered His execution, was astounded when He heard that Christ had died so soon (Mark 15:44).

It was imperative that Christ be dead early enough in the day so that He could be put in the grave some time on Friday. That day had to be included as one of the three days He would be in the earth (the others being Saturday and Sunday).

1. The preparation

As Jesus yielded up His life He said, "It is finished" (John 19:30), and, "Father, into thy hands I commend my spirit" (Luke 23:46). He who controlled life also controlled death. He who could raise Himself from the dead also willed His own death and Himself into the Father's presence.

a) Its importance

John 19:31 begins, "The Jews, therefore, because it was the preparation." By "the Jews," the apostle John had in mind the Jewish leaders who were hostile to Christ, not the Jewish people. The Greek word translated "preparation" (*paraskeuē*) refers to the day before the Sabbath, or Friday. It was called the day of preparation because Exodus 16:23-30 instructed the Jewish people to keep the Sabbath holy. That meant that any food required on the Sabbath had to be prepared the day before. When God provided manna, the people had to collect enough food on Friday to eat on Saturday. Thus Friday became known as the day of preparation for the Sabbath.

b) Its implications

(1) No body could remain on a cross

John 19:31 continues, "The bodies should not remain upon the cross on the sabbath day (for that sabbath was an high day)." The statement is another indication that the day of preparation was

10

Friday, for the religious leaders were concerned that the bodies of criminals not be exposed on the Sabbath. But this wasn't just any Sabbath—it was "an high day," a Passover Sabbath. The Jewish leaders were sure to obey all the rules and regulations on Passover. They derived this particular rule from Deuteronomy 21:22-23, which says, "If a man have committed a sin worthy of death, and he be put to death, and thou hang him on a tree, his body shall not remain all night upon the tree, but thou shalt surely bury him that day (for he who is hanged is accursed by God), that thy land be not defiled." Apparently they didn't always follow that regulation, for historians tell us that bodies were often left on crosses for days. But on this Passover they made sure to perform this particular injunction to the limit.

(2) Death needed to be hastened

The bodies could be removed only after they were dead, and death wasn't likely to occur so soon, for those being crucified had been on the cross for only six hours. That's why the Jewish leaders "besought Pilate that their legs might be broken" (John 19:31). The Greek word translated "broken" means "to smash to pieces." The Romans used a large wooden mallet to smash the legs of the victims until their bones were nothing but splinters. That caused the body weight to shift onto the two nail wounds in the wrists, resulting in suffocation of the internal organs. When the victim could still use his legs, he could push himself up to breathe. But once his legs were broken, the victim had no way to prevent suffocation. The pain would be excruciating.

Following that, the soldiers would give the victim what the Jewish scholar Alfred Edersheim termed the *"coup de grace"* (lit., "the stroke of mercy"), the death stroke (*The Life and Times of Jesus the Messiah,* 2 vols. [Grand Rapids: Eerdmans, 1953], 2:613). A soldier would ram his spear into the victim's heart. So why did the soldiers also break the

11

victim's legs? Commentators have suggested two reasons. One suggestion is that the pain of the victim's shattered legs would traumatize him, and thus the spear thrust would be somewhat of a relief. Edersheim suggests, on the other hand, that they crushed the legs as an "increase in punishment, by way of compensation for its shortening by the final stroke that followed" (p. 613). The general idea behind the spear thrust and the leg breaking was to cause the victim to die immediately. That way the Jewish leaders could remove the body from the cross and maintain the sacredness of the Sabbath. Yet how inconceivable that they would slaughter the Lord of the Sabbath in an effort to keep the Sabbath! Their twisted thinking was the result of their twisted religious system.

2. The prophecies

   a) Christ's unbroken legs

   John 19:32-33 says, "Then came the soldiers, and broke the legs of the first [one of the thieves crucified with Christ], and of the other who was crucified with him, but when they came to Jesus, and saw that he was dead already, they broke not his legs." Even in His death, prophecy was fulfilled. Psalm 34:20 says explicitly of the dying Savior, "He keepeth all his bones; not one of them is broken." We know that prophecy was intended for Jesus because of the testimony of Scripture. John 19:36 says, "These things were done, that the scripture should be fulfilled, A bone of him shall not be broken."

   b) Christ's pierced side

   John 19:34 says, "One of the soldiers, with a spear, pierced his side, and immediately came there out blood and water." Since the soldiers already knew He was dead, why did they give Christ the death stroke? One answer is in verse 37: "Again, another

12

scripture saith, They shall look on him whom they pierced." That particular Scripture verse is Zechariah 12:10. One prophet said that they wouldn't break His legs; another said that they would pierce Him. They did exactly what God intended, and thus indirectly certified that Jesus was the One of whom the prophets spoke.

Verse 34 tells us that blood and water came out of Christ's pierced side—a sign of death. That fulfilled prophecy from Psalm 69, a psalm that contains prophecies of the crucifixion scene, such as verse 21: "They gave me also gall for my food, and in my thirst they gave me vinegar to drink." Verse 20 says, "Reproach hath broken my heart." Under the intense weight of all the sins of everyone who ever lived or will live, it is not inconceivable that a human heart could rupture.

The spear thrust was so deep that Christ could say to Thomas, "Reach here thy hand, and thrust it into my side; and be not faithless, but believing" (John 20:27). When Thomas needed assurance that he was observing the risen Christ, Jesus gave it to him.

Once it was proven that Jesus was dead, His body had to be removed from the cross. But who would care for His body? The disciples had fled. We're not sure that the apostle John was still in the vicinity (cf. John 19:26). The women (Mary the mother of Jesus, Mary Magdalene, Mary the mother of James and Joses, and the mother of Zebedee's children) probably didn't have the means to bury Christ— they were from Galilee, a poor area. Whoever was going to care for the body would have to do so quickly. His body had to be in the grave by 6:00 P.M. on Friday so that the prophecy concerning His being in the earth three days could be fulfilled.

B. God's Man (vv. 57b-60)

1. His identification (v. 57b-c)

13

a) As a rich man (v. 57*b*)

"There came a rich man of Arimathaea, named Joseph."

(1) His characteristics

He was more than just a rich man. Mark 15:43 says he was a "prominent member of the Council [the Sanhedrin]" (NASB)—the Jewish ruling body that sentenced Jesus Christ to death for claiming to be the Son of God. The verse also says that he anticipated the kingdom of God. He had a heart for God's truth. Luke 23:50 tells us he was a good and just man. Verse 51 says he did not consent to condemn Jesus to death. But most importantly he was wealthy—a fulfillment of Isaiah 53:9.

(2) His home

Matthew 27:57 tells us Joseph was from Arimathea. The only thing we know about Arimathea is that it was "a city of the Jews" (Luke 23:51). We assume it was close to the city of Jerusalem, since Joseph's own grave was just outside the city. We assume he wouldn't have lived far from there.

b) As a disciple of Christ (v. 57*c*)

"Who also himself was Jesus' disciple."

A better translation of the Greek text is that he was "discipled by Jesus." He had become a follower of Jesus. The verb in the text means "to be a learner." He was learning from Jesus, believing what He said. John 19:38 gives us additional information about his relationship with Jesus: he was "a disciple of Jesus, but secretly for fear of the Jews." Up to this time Joseph had been a secret disciple because he was afraid of the leaders and what they might do to him if they found out.

Joseph had to act fast because Jesus had to be buried before the Sabbath began on Friday night. So far the Jewish leaders were performing their role in God's plan—they were in a hurry to get Him down from the cross. Pilate could have left Jesus hanging on the cross, but he honored their request because he didn't want to offend them. He'd been blackmailed enough by them in the past (John 19:12).

How Many Days Was Christ Dead?

Some people have difficulty reconciling what Jesus says in Matthew 12:40 about the length of His stay in the grave: "As Jonah was three days and three nights in the belly of the great fish, so shall the Son of man be three days and three nights in the heart of the earth." Does that mean Jesus had to be in the earth three full days and nights? No. Many commentators take that view and place the crucifixion on a Thursday, counting the three days and nights as being Thursday, Friday, and Saturday, with His rising on Sunday. The obvious problem with such a view is that we are left with a fourth-day resurrection. Yet all the passages in Scripture dealing with this issue indicate that Christ was to rise on the third day. That eliminates the need for interpreting Matthew 12:40 as referring to three twenty-four-hour periods. The phrase "three days and three nights" was simply an idiom of the Jewish people referring to a three-day period.

For example, if you were to say, "I'm going to San Diego for three days," does that mean you'll be there for three twenty-four-hour periods? Not necessarily. You may be there for only a few hours one day, all day the next day, and a few hours the third day. That is how Scripture refers to Christ's burial.

In Luke 24:21 the disciples traveling the road to Emmaus were bemoaning the death of Christ, saying, "We hoped that it had been he who should have redeemed Israel; and, besides all this, today [Sunday] is the third day since these things were done." They understood that the Lord's prophecy of His resurrection wasn't going to take place after three twenty-four-hour periods, but on the third day, which from Friday would be Sunday. After all, Jesus said He would "be killed, and be raised again the third day" (Matt. 16:21). Matthew 17:23 repeats, "They shall kill him, and the third day he shall be raised again." The chronological, historical references to the death of Christ indicate a third-day resurrection, not one following three twenty-four-hour periods. When Jesus referred to three days and three nights, we can conclude He was referring to a part of three twenty-four-hour periods. Rabbi Eleazar ben Azariah (who lived around A.D. 100) said, "A day and night are an Onah [a portion of time] and the portion of an Onah is as the whole of it" (Jerusalem Talmud, *Shabbath* ix.3; cf. Babylonian Talmud *Pesahim* 4a).

2. His commitment (v. 58)

"He went to Pilate, and begged the body of Jesus. Then Pilate commanded the body to be delivered."

a) A high price

Joseph was taking a great risk when he did that. He didn't know what Pilate might do to him. After all, Pilate had had enough of the Jewish leaders, who had blackmailed him with their threats to report him to Caesar if he didn't crucify Jesus. Furthermore, because he was a member of the Sanhedrin, the body of leaders who wanted Jesus dead, Joseph would have had to explain why he wanted the body. In addition, since he wasn't a member of Jesus' family, what could Joseph have said to convince Pilate to give him the body, other than that he was a follower of Him? There was no good reason for Joseph to have expected to receive the body.

Joseph surely realized that once word got out that he intended to bury Jesus Christ, and that he was himself a disciple, he would have lost his reputation and social standing. His actions may have put him in a situation where he no longer could do business with people. The price of his commitment was extremely high.

b) A deep love

Joseph was committed to a man who was dead and not yet risen. That is a remarkable commitment. He

16

was so convinced that Jesus was who He claimed to be that he stepped out in faith and courageously gave Jesus the dignified burial He deserved. Joseph was drawn by his love for Christ, even if it meant losing everything he valued in life.

According to Matthew 27:58, Joseph had to beg Pilate for the body of Jesus. Then Pilate commanded that Jesus' body be given to Joseph. Mark 15:44-45 tells us that Pilate was surprised to hear that Jesus had died so soon, and that he therefore checked with a centurion who had been at the scene to verify that Jesus was in fact dead.

3. His actions (vv. 59-60)

   a) He carried the body (v. 59a)

   "When Joseph had taken the body."

   Perhaps Joseph carried Jesus' body himself. According to the latest archaeological discoveries, Joseph's tomb was close to the cross, so he wouldn't have had to carry the body very far. One of the spots believed to be the burial place of Jesus Christ is called "the Garden Tomb," or "Gordon's Calvary." God ensured it was near enough to allow Joseph to bury Christ by Friday night.

   b) He wrapped it in linen (v. 59b)

   "He wrapped it in a clean linen cloth."

   John 19:39-40 tells us another man was with Joseph: Nicodemus (cf. John 3:1-21). Nicodemus was a teacher in Israel, no doubt another member of the Sanhedrin. Both men were prominent in the nation. Verse 39 says that Nicodemus "brought a mixture of myrrh and aloes." The Jewish people didn't embalm their dead; they anointed the body with a heavy load of spices to keep the smell of death from permeating the area until the body was buried. Myrrh was a liquid, and aloes was a powder, and the two were mixed together. Joseph brought fine linen (Matt. 27:59). The women helped Joseph wrap each limb and the torso

17

of Christ's body with the fine linen, and then provided a special napkin for His head.

c) He laid it in the tomb (v. 60a)

"[He] laid it in his own new tomb, which he had hewn out in the rock."

The Garden Tomb was cut by hand out of a wall of rock acting as the face of a low cliff. Just off to its right is another rocky cliff that resembles a skull. Beneath that cliff is a highway where many believe Jesus was crucified. If that indeed is the place, Joseph would have carried Christ's body only a short distance to his tomb.

d) He rolled a stone in front of the tomb (v. 60b)

"He rolled a great stone to the door of the sepulcher, and departed."

The stone was required because of grave robbers. It was a common practice for people to be buried with their belongings, some of which were valuable. Furthermore, the body had to be protected from animals and birds. Today at the Garden Tomb is a great trough holding a huge circular stone that can be rolled across the entrance.

The burial was accomplished before the end of Friday. Matthew 27:62 says, "Now the next day, that followed the day of preparation." Jesus was in the grave before that next day, Saturday, so the prophecy would be fulfilled when He rose on Sunday, the third day. The events surrounding the burial of Jesus Christ were orchestrated by God to fulfill specific prophecy. Christ would be three days in a wealthy man's grave.

I don't know what caused Joseph of Arimathea to publicly manifest himself as a follower of Jesus Christ. Perhaps it was the earthquake, the darkness, the opening of the graves, and the ripping from top to bottom of the veil of the Temple (Matt. 27:45, 51-54). Perhaps it was simply his love for Jesus and the agony he felt watching Him endure pain and suffering on the cross. One thing we can be sure of: God worked on his heart to bring to pass the fulfillment of prophecy.

II. THE TWO MARYS (v. 61)

A. Their Description (v. 61a)

"There were Mary Magdalene and the other Mary."

Mary Magdalene came from Magdala, a village on the west coast of the Sea of Galilee. The other Mary was the mother of James and Joseph (v. 56). John 19:25 calls her the wife of Clopas, or Alphaeus. (Matthew 10:3 refers to James as the son of Alphaeus to differentiate him from James the son of Zebedee.) She was one of the women who followed Him from Galilee to attend to His physical needs by providing food and sustenance. Other women had been present during the crucifixion and burial, but they apparently left with Joseph and Nicodemus (v. 60). Only these two women remained.

B. Their Significance (v. 61b)

"[They were] sitting over against [opposite] the sepulcher."

They were probably in deep sorrow and agony. If Joseph of Arimathea was used by God to confirm the deity of Christ through fulfilled prophecy, these two women were used to affirm the same through firsthand testimony.

1. They saw the evidence

Matthew 28:1-5 says, "In the end of the sabbath, as it began to dawn toward the first day of the week, came Mary Magdalene and the other Mary to see the sepulcher. And, behold, there was a great earthquake; for an angel of the Lord descended from heaven, and came and rolled back the stone from the door, and sat upon it. His countenance was like lightning; and his raiment white as snow; and for fear of him the keepers [Roman guards] did shake, and became as dead men. And the angel answered and said unto the women, Fear not."

These two women felt the ground shake and heard the angel. We do not worship someone we hope came out of the grave—we have eyewitnesses who saw the empty tomb, evidence that the resurrection had occurred.

2. They were commanded to give testimony

The angel continued, "I know that ye seek Jesus, who was crucified. He is not here; for he is risen, as he said. Come, see the place where the Lord lay. And go quickly, and tell his disciples that he is risen from the dead" (vv. 5-7). These two women were given the command to give testimony to the resurrection of Christ. Verse 8 says that they ran "to bring his disciples word."

3. They met the resurrected Christ

Verses 9-10 say, "And as they went to tell his disciples, behold, Jesus met them, saying, All hail. And they came and held him by the feet, and worshiped him. Then said Jesus unto them, Be not afraid; go tell my brethren."

God used two women who couldn't bear to part with Christ for very long. They left the tomb for a time on the Sabbath day, but they came back that third day. They saw the evidence of His resurrection, and God used them to give testimony to what they saw. However feeble their faith may have been, it certainly was stronger than that of the disciples. Some people believe the disciples fabricated the account of the resurrection to carry on their program, but the disciples didn't see the evidence first; the women did (Luke 24:1-12; John 20:1-10). The truth is that the disciples were reluctant to believe what the women said (Luke 24:6-12). Thomas was reluctant to believe when he heard from the other disciples who had seen their risen Lord (John 20:24-25). So God gave us firsthand witnesses to spread the word of the resurrection. Through eyewitness testimony and fulfilled prophecy in the burial of Christ, God was at work vindicating Jesus Christ as His Son.

Focusing on the Facts

1. What is the greatest miracle the world will ever know (see p. 8)?
2. What two prophecies had to be fulfilled in the burial of Jesus Christ (see p. 9)?
3. Whom did God use to fulfill those two prophecies (see p. 9)?
4. Why did Christ have to be buried before the end of Friday (see p. 10)?
5. What is the day of preparation (see p. 10)?
6. Why did the Jewish leaders ask Pilate to break the legs of Jesus and the two criminals who were crucified with Him (see p. 11)?
7. Why didn't the Roman soldiers break Christ's legs (John 19:32-33; 36; see p. 12)?
8. Why did the soldiers thrust a spear into Christ's side (John 19:37; see pp. 12-13)?
9. Describe Joseph of Arimathea (see p. 14).
10. How can you reconcile Matthew 12:40 with the other prophecies that say Jesus would rise on the third day (see pp. 15-16)?
11. What did Joseph risk when he stepped forward to claim the body of Jesus (see p. 16)?
12. Why was it important that Joseph's tomb be close to the site of Christ's crucifixion (see p. 17)?
13. Who helped Joseph with the preparations for Christ's burial (see p. 17)?
14. Describe the two Marys who remained across from the entrance to Christ's tomb (see p. 19).
15. How did God use those two women to confirm the deity of Christ (Matt. 28:1-10; see pp. 19-20)?

Pondering the Principles

1. Isaiah 53 is a moving characterization of Christ's death on the cross. It precisely describes how our Lord felt on the cross. Another chapter like it is Psalm 22. Read both. Record all the words and phrases that describe how Christ felt and how He looked. Meditate on them. Ask God to help you better understand the pain and suffering that Christ endured on your behalf. Then memorize 1 Peter 2:24-25: "He Himself bore our sins in His body on the cross, that we might die to sin and live to righteous-

ness; for by His wounds you were healed. For you were continually straying like sheep, but now you have returned to the Shepherd and Guardian of your souls" (NASB).

2. John 19:38 tells us that Joseph was a disciple of Christ, "but secretly for fear of the Jews." That means that when he stepped forward to claim the body of Christ, he exposed himself as a follower. To be a true follower of Jesus Christ requires that you be identified with Jesus. Besides your Sunday visits to church to worship God, how else do people see your commitment to Christ? Joseph exposed himself as a follower of Christ probably at a great cost to himself. What has following Christ cost you? Read Matthew 16:24-26. Are you trying to save your life, or have you found your life because you lost it for Christ's sake? Step out in faith and be identified with Christ!

2
The Amazing Burial of Jesus Christ
—Part 2

Outline

Introduction
A. God's Sovereignty in Scripture
B. God's Sovereignty in Action
   1. Through miracles
   2. Through providence
     a) The testimony of Scripture
       (1) Proverbs 16:1
       (2) Proverbs 19:21
       (3) Jeremiah 10:23
       (4) Philippians 2:13
       (5) Proverbs 16:9
       (6) John 5:17
     b) The testimony of God's servants
       (1) Joseph
         (*a*) The decision of his brothers
         (*b*) The decision of Potiphar's wife
         (*c*) The decision of Pharaoh
         (*d*) The decision of Joseph
       (2) Ruth
       (3) Esther
         (*a*) The setting
         (*b*) The plot
         (*c*) The deliverance

Review
  I. Joseph of Arimathea (vv. 57-60)
 II. The Two Marys (v. 61)

Lesson
III. The Chief Priests and the Pharisees (vv. 62-66)
   A. The Context of the Scene (v. 62)
      1. An important day (v. 62a)
      2. An uncommon alliance (v. 62b)
   B. The Command of the Leaders (vv. 63-64)
      1. Subvert a prophetical claim (v. 63)
         a) The leaders' contempt
         b) The leaders' concern
      2. Eliminate a potential fabrication (v. 64a)
      3. Avoid a permanent deception (v. 64b)
   C. The Complacency of Pilate (v. 65)
   D. The Consequence of Providence (v. 66)

Conclusion

Introduction

One of the greatest and most essential attributes of God is His sovereignty, sometimes referred to as the supremacy of God. God rules over all things and controls all things. The ramifications of this doctrine are beyond our ability to comprehend, yet it is essential that we realize its truth. The Bible teaches unequivocally that God is the supreme ruler in the universe.

A. God's Sovereignty in Scripture

   1. 1 Chronicles 29:11-13—"Thine, O Lord, is the greatness, and the power, and the glory, and the victory, and the majesty; for all that is in the heaven and in the earth is thine. Thine is the kingdom, O Lord, and thou art exalted as head above all. Both riches and honor come of thee, and thou reignest over all; and in thine hand is power and might; and in thine hand it is to make great, and to give strength unto all. Now therefore, our God, we thank thee, and praise thy glorious name."

   2. 2 Chronicles 20:6—"O Lord God of our fathers, art not thou God in heaven? And rulest not thou over all the kingdoms of the nations? And in thine hand is there not power and might, so that none is able to withstand thee?"

24

3. Job 23:13—"He is of one mind, and who can turn him? And what his soul desireth, even that he doeth." God never vacillates between opinions.

4. Psalm 115:3—"Our God is in the heavens; he hath done whatsoever he hath pleased."

5. Psalm 135:6—"Whatsoever the Lord pleased, that did he in heaven, and in earth, in the seas, and all deep places."

6. Proverbs 21:30—"There is no wisdom, nor understanding, nor counsel against the Lord."

7. Isaiah 46:10—"My counsel shall stand, and I will do all my pleasure."

8. Daniel 4:35—"[God] doeth according to his will in the army of heaven, and among the inhabitants of the earth, and none can stay his hand, or say unto him, What doest thou?"

9. Ephesians 1:11—"[He] worketh all things after the counsel of his own will."

B. God's Sovereignty in Action

Those verses tell us that God is in charge. All the billions of isolated circumstances in the world do not function at random. The designer has a purpose and objective for each one. It's enough for us to understand how rapidly a computer can come to a conclusion based on identifiable data. But to understand how the infinite mind of God can collect, collate, and harmonize every bit of data that exists in the universe and make it all work for His will is beyond our comprehension. To get a small grasp on that reality we need to realize two ways that God rules in the world.

1. Through miracles

At times God supernaturally interrupts the natural course of events to accomplish His purpose. He overrules natural law with supernatural power. There is no scientific explanation for a miracle.

a) Creation was the greatest miracle of all—God created everything that exists in only six days (Gen. 1).

b) Another miracle was a cataclysmic flood—God drowned the entire world except for eight people and two of each kind of animal (Gen. 6-8).

c) Many supernatural plagues descended on Egypt, including the death of the firstborn of everyone who didn't believe in God (Ex. 5-13). God miraculously overruled the course of nature to lead His people out of Egypt and into the Promised Land.

d) God parted the Red Sea for the people of Israel to pass through, then allowed it to drown the armies of Egypt who followed in pursuit (Ex. 14).

e) God brought water from a rock (Ex. 17:1-6).

f) God provided manna from heaven and birds to eat when the people desired meat (Ex. 16:1-13).

g) On one occasion God caused the shadow of the sun to go backwards on a sundial (2 Kings 20:8-11).

h) On another occasion God caused the sun to stand still, which means that the earth stopped revolving. Amazingly enough, that didn't result in total destruction (Josh. 10:12-14).

i) During the rebellion of Korah, God allowed the ground to open up and swallow all who rebelled against Him (Num. 16). The miracle was that the ground swallowed only those who had sinned and not the others.

j) The walls of Jericho fell down—apart from any natural phenomena—thus permitting Israel's army to enter the city (Josh. 7).

k) Samson had such incredible strength that he was able to kill thousands of his enemies (Judg. 15-16).

l) Working through the prophet Elisha, God made an ax head float (2 Kings 6).

m) Working through the prophet Elija, God raised a dead boy (1 Kings 17:17-23).

n) God miraculously provided food for a widow (1 Kings 17:8-16).

o) On one occasion a donkey talked (Num. 22).

p) God took Elijah to heaven without his dying. He caught him up in a whirlwind in a "chariot of fire" (2 Kings 2:11).

q) During King Belshazzar's feast, handwriting miraculously appeared on a wall (Dan. 5).

r) God closed up the mouths of lions to prevent them from eating the prophet Daniel (Dan. 6).

s) Three men—Shadrach, Meshach, and Abednego—were not even singed after being thrown into a fiery furnace (Dan. 3).

t) The prophet Jonah survived for three days in the belly of a great fish (Jonah 1-2).

Then there are the healings wrought by Jesus and the miracles of the apostles. At times God has accomplished His eternal purposes in ways that interrupt the flow of natural history.

2. Through providence

God also uses providence to accomplish His will in the world. You won't find the word *providence* in the Bible. It's like the word *Trinity*—the word isn't in the Bible, but the theological concept is. Rather than overruling or interrupting the natural course of events, God manipulates and uses those events to accomplish His own ends. That's what is meant by the providence of God.

In a sense, providence is a greater miracle than a miracle. It seems to me easier for God to instantly overrule the natural flow of events than to use a diverse number of events, circumstances, and attitudes occurring within the limited freedom of men and demons to accomplish His will. But that is precisely what God does! That's why the psalmist says He has power over all.

a) The testimony of Scripture

Throughout the Bible you can find God using thunder, lightning, rain, hail, frost, ice, snow, cold, heat, sunshine, bodies of water, rivers, animals, birds, beasts, nations, governments, kings, princes, rulers, and governors—He uses everything and everyone to meet His desires. The seemingly random choices we make may appear to be detached from any sovereign control, yet God sets the birth and death of every man. He sees all we do, think, and say. He uses our good and our bad. He uses the free choices of men— and even demons—to fit perfectly into His eternal purposes.

(1) Proverbs 16:1—"The plans of the heart belong to man, but the answer of the tongue is from the Lord" (NASB).

(2) Proverbs 19:21—"There are many devices in a man's heart; nevertheless, the counsel of the Lord, that shall stand."

(3) Jeremiah 10:23—"The way of man is not in himself; it is not in man that walketh to direct his steps." Men believe they're doing what they want to do, but the fact is that what they do fits into a grander scheme.

(4) Philippians 2:13—The apostle Paul said, "It is God who worketh in you both to will and to do of his good pleasure." He controls everything— even sin. He allows some, prevents some, and limits it for His purpose.

(5) Proverbs 16:9—"A man's heart deviseth his way, but the Lord directeth his steps."

(6) John 5:17—Jesus said, "My Father worketh hitherto, and I work." Even though He was on earth, He affirmed that they were still working in concert to bring about God's eternal plan.

Most of the time God does not use miracles to accomplish His will. He did use them in the days of Moses, Elijah and Elisha, Christ, and the apostles. Only during those four periods of redemptive history do we see miracles as anything near the norm. The remainder of the time God uses providence.

b) The testimony of God's servants

(1) Joseph

(*a*) The decision of his brothers

Joseph was one of twelve brothers. His brothers hated him because he was the favorite son, so they decided to kill him (Gen. 37:20). But after noticing a group of traders traveling to Egypt, they decided to sell Joseph into slavery instead (v. 27).

(*b*) The decision of Potiphar's wife

In Egypt Joseph became the servant of a man named Potiphar (Gen. 39:1). Potiphar's wife liked the way Joseph looked, so she decided to seduce him. But Joseph didn't want to have anything to do with her, so he ran (vv. 6-12). She grabbed his coat as he ran, and then falsely accused him of intending to rape her. Joseph was then thrown into prison (vv. 13-20).

(*c*) The decision of Pharaoh

While in jail, Joseph met a prisoner who had an unusual dream. Joseph interpreted his dream (Gen. 40:1-19). Later, Pharaoh had a dream and asked if anyone could interpret it for him (Gen. 41:1-8). He was told that Joseph could interpret his dream (vv. 9-13). So Joseph was brought before Pharaoh and interpreted the dream; as a consequence, Pharaoh made him prime minister of Egypt (vv. 14-44).

So far in this story there have been no miracles. The decision of the brothers, the decision of Potiphar's wife, and the decision of Pharaoh have led Joseph from being sold into slavery to becoming the second in command of all Egypt.

(d) The decision of Joseph

Joseph's interpretation of Pharaoh's dream indicated that seven years of plenty would be followed by seven years of famine. During the seven years of plenty, Joseph collected a 20 percent tax from the people of all their food and grain and stored it to feed the nation during the seven years of famine (vv. 34-35, 48-49). As the seven years of famine began, the people in Joseph's homeland soon ran out of food. So they came to Egypt to beg for food (Gen. 41:57–42:2). But to get that food they had to go to Joseph.

If Joseph's family had not gone to Egypt, they would have perished in Canaan. And that would have been the end of the twelve tribes of Israel. Genesis 45:4-5 records what eventually happened when the brothers came to Joseph: "Joseph said unto his brethren, Come near to me, I pray you. And they came near. And he said, I am Joseph, your brother, whom ye sold into Egypt. Now therefore be not grieved, nor angry with yourselves, that ye sold me here; for God did send me before you to preserve life."

God could have picked up Joseph in a cloud, dropped him into Egypt, and instantly made him prime minister. That would have been a miracle. But God didn't use a miracle; He used providence. The seemingly random choices of many people accomplished God's perfect plan. Joseph further explained God's purpose, "For these two years hath the famine been in the land: and yet there are five years, in which there shall neither be plowing nor harvest. And God sent me before you to preserve you a posterity in the earth, and to save your lives by a great deliverance. So now it was not you that sent me here, but God" (vv. 6-8). In Genesis 50:20 Joseph concludes, "You meant evil against me, but God meant it for good" (NASB).

(2) Ruth

Naomi's son violated the law of God by marrying a pagan Moabite woman named Ruth. They lived with his mother, brother, and sister-in-law in Moab for ten years (Ruth 1:4). Then he and his brother died, perhaps as a result of divine judgment, leaving Naomi with her two daughters-in-law (v. 5). As a result of Naomi's testimony, Ruth said, "Thy people shall be my people, and thy God, my God" (v. 16). She came to faith in the true God. Out of the sin of a disobedient man God brought Ruth and Naomi together, which resulted in Ruth's salvation. Naomi took Ruth back to her land (v. 19). One day Ruth was gleaning in the field of a man named Boaz, who was related to her dead husband (Ruth 2:1-2). Under Jewish law Boaz could take Ruth as his wife, which he did (Ruth 4:9-10). She became the grandmother of David, putting her in the messianic line (vv. 21-22). There was no miracle, just providence.

(3) Esther

One of the most striking illustrations of God's providence in the Old Testament is the book of

Esther. Surprisingly enough, the book of Esther never mentions the name of God. Yet clearly the main character in the book of Esther is God. No miracles are recorded in the book, but God is at work in a way even beyond the miraculous. In an incredible series of providential events, God brought about His will. And in this case, His will was to preserve the nation of Israel.

(a) The setting

The setting is the kingdom of Persia, where the Jewish people had been taken in exile. The book begins by chronicling the deposing of Vashti, the queen (1:10-22). The king wanted a replacement for Vashti, and he wanted her to be the most beautiful woman in the kingdom (2:1-4). As it happened, a Jewish man named Mordecai was foster father to a beautiful niece, Esther. He was a keeper of the king's gate (2:19), and he realized that the king's command that a new queen be found might be a wonderful opportunity for Esther to live in the palace of the king and be a good influence. So Esther entered the beauty contest and won (2:16-17).

(b) The plot

No one knew Esther was Jewish—Mordecai had instructed her to tell no one (2:10). Meanwhile, a high official named Haman persuaded the king to issue an edict commanding the annihilation of the Jewish people (3:8-11). Haman was actually seeking to kill Mordecai, whose devotion to God offended him (3:5).

(c) The deliverance

Esther found out about the plot. Since she was in a position to influence the king, she pleaded with him on behalf of her people (7:1-6). The king favored Esther and Mordecai,

32

spared the Jewish race, made Mordecai the prime minister, and hanged Haman on the gallows Haman had built for Mordecai (7:7–8:17). Thus the nation of Israel was preserved. God was in control of every single event.

Despite those incredible illustrations of God's providence, no more graphic account in all Scripture of God's sovereignty exists than the death of Jesus Christ. God used human and satanic forces combined to kill His Son. He controlled the hatred of the Jewish leaders, the hostility of the Romans toward those leaders, the defection of the disciples, the betrayal of Judas, and the denial of Peter. Jesus came into Jerusalem on the very day Daniel prophesied He would (Dan. 9:25; cf. Harold W. Hoehner, *Chronological Aspects of the Life of Christ* [Grand Rapids: Zondervan, 1977], pp. 115-39). While the people were selecting their Passover lamb, He came as the true Passover Lamb. He died on the very day the Passover lambs were slaughtered. Every single detail was covered. And it was all accomplished by the free choice of evil men and demons. But even that was the work of God.

Acts 4:27-28 says, "Against thy holy child, Jesus, whom thou hast anointed, both Herod, and Pontius Pilate, with the nations, and the people of Israel, were gathered together, to do whatever thy hand and thy counsel determined before to be done." With their own independent choices and within the framework of their sin, they all did what God laid out for them to do. As Psalm 76:10 says, "Surely the wrath of men shall praise thee."

Review

In the burial of Christ we see the providence of God at work. He accomplishes His will through three groups of people.

I. JOSEPH OF ARIMATHEA (vv. 57-60; see pp. 8-19)

Joseph was the man God used to fulfill two prophecies: that He would be with a rich man in His death (Isa. 53:9) and that He would be three days in the earth before His resurrection (Matt. 12:40).

II. THE TWO MARYS (v. 61; see pp. 19-20)

Mary Magdalene and Mary the mother of James and Joseph were used by God to affirm the deity of Christ by giving testimony of the evidence of the resurrection.

Lesson

III. THE CHIEF PRIESTS AND THE PHARISEES (vv. 62-66)

A. The Context of the Scene (v. 62)

1. An important day (v. 62a)

"Now the next day, that followed the day of the preparation."

That's a roundabout way of saying it was the Sabbath. The day of preparation was always Friday. All the meal planning had to be done in advance because the people weren't allowed to do any work on the Sabbath. This particular Sabbath was special—it was a Passover Sabbath, the holiest day of all in the Jewish calendar.

2. An uncommon alliance (v. 62b)

"The chief priests and Pharisees came together unto Pilate."

The chief priests and Pharisees represent the Sanhedrin, the religious ruling body in Israel. The chief priests were Sadducees, and the Sadducees and Pharisees were theological enemies who had little to do with one another—except on one other occasion (Matt. 21:45-46). The one thing they could agree on was the need to eliminate Jesus Christ. Yet it wasn't enough for Him to be dead; they were afraid of one more thing. So they formed a contingent to meet with Pilate.

The phrase "came together unto Pilate" probably should be read as indicating that the contingent met the ruler in the praetorium or palace. The day before, when

34

they brought Jesus to Pilate, they sent Jesus in alone. They didn't accompany Him because they didn't want to be defiled for the Passover by entering a Gentile dwelling (John 18:28). Apparently this was a clandestine visit. As long as there was no one to see that the leaders were violating their own rules, they went right in. They also were on an important mission from their standpoint, so they weren't concerned about legalism. Murderers don't hold ceremony in high regard. They hated Jesus more than they loved their own law, so they violated it.

B. The Command of the Leaders (vv. 63-64)

1. Subvert a prophetical claim (v. 63)

"Sir, we remember that that deceiver said, while he was yet alive, After three days I will rise again."

a) The leaders' contempt

The leaders referred to Jesus as "that deceiver." The pronoun translated "that" indicates their desire to keep Him far removed from themselves. Then they called Him a "deceiver"—a seducer of the people. They held Christ in great contempt. Their hatred extended even beyond His death.

b) The leaders' concern

The chief priests and Pharisees were concerned about Christ's claim that He would rise again after three days. He gave them that prophecy after certain scribes and Pharisees asked for a sign (Matt. 12:38). Jesus replied, "An evil and adulterous generation seeketh after a sign, and there shall no sign be given to it, but the sign of the prophet, Jonah; for as Jonah was three days and three nights in the belly of the great fish, so shall the Son of man be three days and three nights in the heart of the earth" (vv. 39-40). They understood what He meant. Jonah went into the fish and then came out. They knew that Jesus was saying that He would be buried and then rise again. Even the disciples didn't understand that

35

much—they thought He was talking figuratively. They didn't realize He was speaking of His literal death and resurrection (John 20:9). Nevertheless, the Jewish leaders wanted to prevent any rumors of resurrection from springing up.

2. Eliminate a potential fabrication (v. 64*a*)

"Command, therefore, that the sepulcher be made sure until the third day, lest his disciples come by night, and steal him away, and say unto the people, He is risen from the dead."

The Jewish leaders were still giving orders to Pilate. He continued to be intimidated by his fear of their reporting him to Caesar in the case of another conflict. The leaders weren't afraid Christ would rise; they were afraid the disciples would fabricate a resurrection to keep the movement alive. The irony is that the disciples had no such thought. They were afraid to do anything, let alone recognize the importance of the resurrection of Christ to their movement.

Jesus' Teaching About the Resurrection in the Gospel of Mark

Jesus taught the disciples about His resurrection many times. He taught them in Matthew 16:21, 17:23, and 20:19; and on numerous occasions in Mark He taught His disciples this fundamental truth.

1. Mark 8:31—"He began to teach them, that the Son of man must suffer many things, and be rejected by the elders, and by the chief priests, and scribes, and be killed, and after three days rise again." Amazingly enough, Peter then rebuked Him (v. 32).

2. Mark 9:9-10—"As they came down from the mountain [after the transfiguration], he charged them that they should tell no man what things they had seen, till the Son of man were risen from the dead. And they kept that saying to themselves, questioning one with another what the rising from the dead should mean." The disciples couldn't handle that teaching because they couldn't believe He would ever die.

3. Mark 9:31-32—"He taught his disciples and said unto them, The Son of man is delivered into the hands of men, and they shall kill him; and after he is killed, he shall rise the third day. But they understood not that saying, and were afraid to ask him."

4. Mark 10:33—Jesus said, "Behold, we go up to Jerusalem; and the Son of man shall be delivered unto the chief priests, and unto the scribes; and they shall condemn him to death, and shall deliver him to the Gentiles. And they shall mock him, and shall scourge him, and shall spit upon him, and shall kill him; and the third day he shall rise again."

The disciples still didn't understand His teaching. John 20:9 says that after Peter and John saw the empty tomb, "as yet they knew not the scripture, that he must rise again from the dead."

3. Avoid a permanent deception (v. 64b)

"The last error shall be worse than the first."

They considered the first error to be Jesus' triumphal entry. Jesus came riding into the city on a colt, fulfilling prophecy (Matt. 21:2-5; Zech. 9:9). The people laid out their garments and branches before Him (v. 8). As Jesus rode into the city, the people cried out, "Hosanna to the Son of David! Blessed is he that cometh in the name of the Lord! Hosanna in the highest" (v. 9)! They showered on Jesus all the messianic accolades. The whole city went out to Jesus, believing He was the Messiah. The Jewish leaders saw the incident as a tremendous deception.

The leaders threatened Pilate that if the first deception caused such an uproar, there would be even greater problems if the disciples were able to fabricate Christ's resurrection. That's why they commanded Pilate to put a guard around the tomb to prevent the disciples from stealing the body.

C. The Complacency of Pilate (v. 65)

"Pilate said unto them, Ye have a watch [or, "Take a watch"]; go your way, make it as sure as you can."

37

He gave them a Roman guard. Pilate wanted only to brush this problem away. He had had enough of their commands by now.

D. The Consequence of Providence (v. 66)

"So they went, and made the sepulcher secure, sealing the stone, and setting a watch."

Sealing the stone doesn't mean they sealed it with glue. They probably put some wax on the stone and on the wall of the cave, and then ran some string through the wax. If anyone moved the stone, they would break the string. Thus the Romans would have known if someone had tampered with the tomb. The wax itself may have been stamped with a Roman imprimatur so that the offender would know he was violating Roman law. Additionally, a group of Roman soldiers was set as a guard in front of the grave. The tomb was extremely secure.

Some people today still believe that the disciples stole the body of Christ. But Matthew 27:66 proves that they didn't. God made sure that a group of Christ's enemies made the grave secure. There was no way the disciples or anyone else could have stolen Christ's body. The only way Christ could have come out of the grave was by the resurrection. Once again God used the wrath of men to praise Him.

If there had been no guard to watch the tomb, and if no seal had been set upon it, we would have great difficulty in preaching a message that Jesus rose from the dead without someone's claiming it never happened. They could get away with saying that the disciples took His body and that someone took on Christ's identity and made a few appearances. But the unbelieving world itself made sure that there's no possible explanation for the missing body of Jesus Christ other than the resurrection. Later, in Matthew 28:11-15, the guards were bribed to deny the resurrection—another testimony to its reality.

Conclusion

God used Joseph of Arimathea to fulfill prophecy. He used the two Marys to give firsthand testimony to the empty tomb, evidence of the resurrection. And He used the chief priests and Pharisees to give forceful proof that Jesus indeed rose from the dead.

How does all this remarkable display of God's providence relate to you and me? Romans 8:28 says, "We know that all things work together for good to them that love God, to them who are the called according to his purpose." All things are controlled by God to work together to fulfill His eternal purpose for His own beloved children. The doctrine of God's sovereignty and providence is not merely for theologians. When you can't explain the trouble you're experiencing, you need to understand the providential power of a sovereign God who controls everything in the universe for your good and His glory. Remember that He demonstrated His ability to do that in the death and burial of Jesus Christ. Everything that happens in your life—including trials—somehow fits into the plan of God. He is in control. He hasn't abandoned His throne. Our hope and confidence are in God, who providentially, and if need be miraculously, controls all things for His own eternal purposes.

Focusing on the Facts

1. What is one of the most essential attributes of God (see p. 24)?
2. What are some of the things Scripture teaches about that attribute (see pp. 24-25)?
3. Cite some examples of how God intervened through miracles (see pp. 25-27).
4. What is the other method God uses to accomplish His will in the world (see p. 27)?
5. What are some of the things God uses to meet His desires (see p. 28)?
6. Cite some Scripture verses that reveal how God uses people to fulfill His plans (see pp. 28-29).
7. Explain how God used Joseph to preserve the twelve tribes of Israel (see pp. 29-31).
8. Explain how God directed circumstances to put Ruth, a Moabite, into the messianic line (see p. 31).

9. Explain how God used Esther to prevent the annihilation of the Jewish race (see pp. 31-33).
10. What does Acts 4:27-28 teach about God's involvement in the death of Jesus Christ (see p. 33)?
11. Why did the chief priests and Pharisees form an alliance to visit Pilate (see p. 34)?
12. What concerned the chief priest and Pharisees about Christ's claim that He would rise the third day (see pp. 35-36)?
13. What did Jesus teach about His resurrection (see pp. 36-37)?
14. What was the first error the Jewish leaders believed Jesus had perpetrated on the people (see p. 37)?
15. What is significant about the fact that Christ's enemies set a seal on His tomb and placed a guard in front of it (see p. 38)?

Pondering the Principles

1. We saw how God providentially led Joseph, Ruth, and Esther to accomplish great things in His eternal plan (see pp. 29-33). Look back on your life both before you were a believer and after. Make a list of the things God did providentially to lead you to Christ. Then make another list of the things God has done to bring you to where you are now in your Christian life. Thank God for how He has led you in the past. Glorify Him as a result of His faithfulness to you.

2. Read Romans 8:28. As a result of this study, how do you plan to view the present and future circumstances you find yourself in? How will you respond when others make decisions that affect your life, whether for good or for bad? Remember to fulfill a key phrase in Romans 8:28, "God causes all things to work together for good *to those who love God, to those who are called according to His purpose*" (NASB, emphasis added).

3
The Resurrection of Jesus Christ—Part 1

Outline

Introduction
A. The Reactions to the Resurrection
B. The Role of the Resurrection
   1. In the gospels
   2. In Acts
   3. In the epistles

Lesson
  I. The Time of the Resurrection (v. 1*a*)
   A. The Day After the Sabbath
   B. The Third Day
 II. The Emotions of the Women (vv. 1*b*-10)
   A. Sympathy (v. 1*b*)
    1. The identity of the women
    2. The intention of the women
     a) Their purpose
     b) Their problem
   B. Terror (vv. 2-7)
    1. The angel's descent (vv. 2-4)
     a) The revelation of the angel (v. 2*a*-*b*)
      (1) The earthquake (v. 2*a*)
      (2) The angel (v. 2*b*)
     b) The role of the angel (vv. 2*c*-3)
      (1) To move the stone (v. 2*c*)
      (2) To attest to the resurrection (v. 2*d*)
      (3) To represent God (v. 3)
     c) The reaction to the angel (v. 4)

2. The angel's explanation (vv. 5-6*b*)
   a) Offered (v. 5*a*)
   b) Examined (vv. 5*b*-6*b*)
      (1) He calmed the women's fears (v. 5*b*)
      (2) He knew the women's objective (v. 5*c*)
      (3) He confirmed Christ's resurrection (v. 6*a*)
      (4) He recalled Christ's prophecy (v. 6*b*)
3. The angel's invitation (v. 6*c*)
4. The angel's command (v. 7)
   a) To exhort the disciples (v. 7*a*)

Conclusion

Introduction

The resurrection of Jesus Christ is the cornerstone of the Christian faith. Everything we are, have, and ever hope to be is predicated on the reality of the resurrection. There would be no Christianity without it (1 Cor. 15:14). Conversely, because Jesus Christ rose from the dead, all elements of our faith are affirmed as true.

A. The Reactions to the Resurrection

There are many possible reactions to the resurrection.

1. Rationalism

   Some reject the resurrection because it does not fit into human reason. This humanistic view assumes that only what can be observed and explained in naturalistic terms can be true. Rationalism rejects the resurrection as it does all other miraculous elements of redemptive history.

2. Unbelief

   Unbelievers don't reason away the reality of the resurrection; they just refuse to believe the truth. Simple unbelief is a denial of what is fact. And the resurrection is perhaps the most indisputable fact in all ancient history, based on reliable evidence and testimony from many witnesses.

3. Doubt

Doubters question the resurrection. There is honest doubt, exhibited by a true seeker desiring to have his questions about the resurrection resolved. Then there is hypocritical doubt, reflected by the person who continues to question long after the available evidence is made clear.

4. Indifference

The indifferent person doesn't care if the resurrection is true or not. He can't see that it makes any claim on his life, and it isn't on his list of priorities. He is simply not interested.

5. Ignorance

Some people are not familiar with the facts of the resurrection. They may not even know about it.

6. Hostility

Some respond out of hostility to the resurrection. They make a vociferous effort to discredit it. A few even see it as their duty to write against the resurrection.

7. Faith

Sadly, all those reactions are wrong and unnecessary. The proper response is faith, belief, affirmation, and application of the reality of the resurrection to one's life.

B. The Role of the Resurrection

1. In the gospels

The four gospels are a response of faith to the resurrection. Matthew, Mark, Luke, and John all believed in the resurrection of Jesus Christ. They weren't forced to believe; they believed because they were overwhelmed with the evidence, as were all who became a part of the believing community. It is the response of faith that we will see in our study of Matthew 28:1-10.

43

Some people are under the illusion that the Bible is a miscellaneous collection of spiritual truths. But every book in the Bible has a specifically designed beginning and ending. In the case of Matthew's gospel, the ending is the glory of the resurrection—the greatest event of all time.

2. In Acts

The first sermon ever preached by the early church was on the resurrection (Acts 2). The reality of the resurrection became the theme of all apostolic preaching. Peter preached on the resurrection in Acts 4 and 10, Stephen preached the resurrection in chapter 7, and Philip preached the resurrection in chapter 8. Paul preached the resurrection many times throughout the rest of the book.

3. In the epistles

The theme of the epistles is the resurrection.

a) Romans 6:4—"Christ was raised up from the dead by the glory of the Father."

b) 1 Corinthians 15:4—"He rose again the third day according to the scriptures."

c) 2 Corinthians 4:14—"He who raised up the Lord Jesus shall raise up us also."

d) Galatians 1:1—"By Jesus Christ, and God the Father, who raised him from the dead."

e) Ephesians 1:20—"Which He [God] wrought in Christ, when he raised him from the dead."

f) Philippians 3:10—Paul said, "That I may know him, and the power of his resurrection."

g) Colossians 2:12—"God . . . raised him from the dead."

h) 1 Thessalonians 1:10—"His Son . . . he [God] raised from the dead."

i) 1 Peter 1:3—"[God] hath begotten us again unto a living hope by the resurrection of Jesus Christ."

The book of Revelation affirms that Christ has right to the earth because He was once dead and is now alive forevermore (1:18). The theme of the New Testament is the resurrection of Jesus Christ.

Here is the foundation of all our hope: Jesus said, "Because I live, ye shall live also" (John 14:19). Jesus also said, "I am the resurrection, and the life; he that believeth in me, though he were dead, yet shall he live. And whosoever liveth and believeth in me shall never die" (John 11:25-26). The resurrection is the core of all we believe.

Each of the four gospel writers presented the resurrection in a unique way, picking out certain elements of the event to reinforce certain spiritual truths in the minds of the readers. As we study Matthew's account of the resurrection, we will draw from Mark, Luke, and John to enrich and fill out the scene so that we may appreciate all its great truth.

Mark, Luke, and John take different approaches, yet all four describe the same historical truth. There is no contradiction—all the facts are in perfect harmony.

Matthew describes the resurrection from the viewpoint of a group of women and the emotions that their actions revealed. That is a wonderful and refreshing way to view the resurrection. We will not coldly analyze the resurrection, but I pray we will feel it. (For a reasoned, apologetic discourse on the resurrection, see chap. 5.)

Lesson

I. THE TIME OF THE RESURRECTION (v. 1*a*)

"In the end of the sabbath, as it began to dawn toward the first day of the week."

A. The Day After the Sabbath

The phrase translated "in the end of the Sabbath" is a unique construction in the Greek text (*opse de sabbatōn*). The best way to translate it is "after the Sabbath." And it would be consistent with the context to translate it "long after the Sabbath." It expresses the idea that a certain interval of time had passed since the Sabbath. The Sabbath ended Saturday at sundown. The next phrase tells us how much time had passed since then: "as it began to dawn toward the first day of the week." The Greek phrase again uses the word *sabbatōn* (Sabbath). The Greek text is literally translated "at day one with reference to the Sabbath." The Jewish people did not give each day a separate name, such as Sunday, Monday, Tuesday, and so on. They named the days numerically with reference to the Sabbath, such as day one after the Sabbath, day two after the Sabbath, day three after the Sabbath, and so on. It was Sunday morning near dawn, and perhaps as many as ten hours passed since the Sabbath.

B. The Third Day

This was the third day the Lord had been in the grave. He was put in the tomb on Friday, was there all day Saturday, and was there a short time on Sunday. Mark 16:2 says, "Very early in the morning of the first day of the week, they came unto the sepulcher at the rising of the sun." Luke 24:1 also says, "Very early in the morning." John 20:1 says, "While it was yet dark."

The stage was set because it was the third day. Many times Jesus said He would rise from the grave on the third day (Matt. 12:40; 16:21; 17:23; 20:19; Mark 9:31; 10:34; Luke 9:22; 18:33; John 2:19-22). And He repeated the prophecy throughout the latter days of His ministry.

Ending an Era of Sabbaths

The Sabbath had been the special day of rest for centuries following creation. But the Sabbath Jesus spent in the grave was the last authorized Sabbath. It was the end of an era of Sabbaths, and the beginning of a new day of worship—the Lord's Day. The nine-teenth-century English preacher Charles Haddon Spurgeon had a wonderful way of explaining the transition. It went something like this: "We gather together on the first rather than upon the seventh day of the week because redemption is even a greater work than creation. Like the apostles, we meet on the first day of the week, and hope that Jesus may stand in our midst, and say, 'Peace be unto you.' Our Lord lifted the Sabbath from the old and rusted hinges whereon the law had placed it long before, and set it on the new golden hinges that His love had fashioned. Instead of placing our day of rest at the end of a week of toil, He placed it at the beginning of the rest that 'remaineth . . . to the people of God' (Heb. 4:9). Every first day of the week we were to meditate upon the rising of our Lord, and seek to enter into fellowship with Him in His risen life." That's why we meet on Sunday, not on the Sabbath.

II. THE EMOTIONS OF THE WOMEN (vv. 1b-10)

A. Sympathy (v. 1b)

"Mary Magdalene and the other Mary [came] to see the sepulcher."

Women have a tremendous capacity to love. The women who came to the tomb that morning loved the Lord Jesus Christ more than anyone. They had ministered with Jesus in Galilee, attending to His needs: they had provided food, hospitality, and even money and resources for Him and His disciples as they carried on the Galilean ministry (Luke 8:1-3). They had journeyed to Jerusalem for the Passover with Jesus and His disciples. They had been with Him at the cross (Matt. 27:56) and when He was buried (27:61). Now they returned on the morning of the third day. They were loyal, devoted, and sympathetic.

1. The identity of the women

Matthew 28:1 identifies Mary Magdalene and Mary, the mother of James and Joseph, and the wife of Clopas or Alphaeus (cf. Matt. 27:56; John 19:25). But they were not alone. Matthew focuses on just those two women. Mark 16:1 adds that Salome, the mother of James and John and the wife of Zebedee, was there (Matt. 27:56). Luke

47

24:10 says that Joanna, the wife of Chuza, who was a steward of Herod (Luke 8:3), was there. John mentioned only Mary Magdalene, but he used the plural pronoun translated "we" in John 20:2.

2. The intention of the women

   a) Their purpose

   Matthew 28:1 tells us they came to see the grave, not the risen Lord. As many times as Jesus had promised the resurrection, their faith could not accept it. Mark 16:1 says, "When the sabbath was past, Mary Magdalene, and Mary, the mother of James, and Salome, had bought sweet spices, that they might come and anoint him." It is possible that the previous night, when the Sabbath ended, some shops might have opened, making it possible for the women to purchase spices. Their purpose was not to see a resurrection but to anoint a corpse.

   John 19:39-40 tells us that Jesus had already been anointed with in excess of seventy pounds of myrrh and aloes and then had been wrapped in linen brought by Joseph of Arimathea. The Jewish people held to a tradition that might explain the women's desire to anoint Christ's body again. They believed that on the fourth day after death the spirit left the body permanently because the body was so decayed. That tradition is seen in Martha's response to the Lord when He wanted her brother Lazarus's tomb opened. She said, "Lord, by this time he stinketh; for he hath been dead four days" (John 11:39). She believed it was too late for Jesus to do anything. Perhaps the four women came on the third day to Jesus' grave because they realized that they had only one more day to anoint Him before His body decayed. One last time they wanted to reach out in love and sympathy to the One they adored. Even though He was dead, they wanted to preserve His body for those last remaining hours.

b) Their problem

Mark 16:3 tells us that as the women walked to the tomb, "they said among themselves, Who shall roll away the stone for us from the door of the sepulcher?" What's more, they had no idea the tomb was being guarded by the Romans, or that it was sealed and couldn't be opened. They anticipated arriving at an empty garden and needing the help of someone to roll the stone from the front of the tomb.

B. Terror (vv. 2-7)

1. The angel's descent (vv. 2-4)

a) The revelation of the angel (v. 2*a-b*)

(1) The earthquake (v. 2*a*)

"Behold, there was a great earthquake."

That was the second earthquake in Jerusalem in three days. When Christ died, an earthquake split rocks open and opened graves (Matt. 27:51-52). In this second earthquake God again demonstrated His presence. But God had previously used earthquakes to mark significant times. There was an earthquake in Exodus 19:18 when God gave Moses the law. In 1 Kings 19:11 God caused an earthquake as He spoke to the prophet Elijah. In the future an earthquake will mark the coming of the Lord (Joel 2:10). Revelation 6, 8, and 11 describe earthquakes related to His return. In His Olivet discourse, Jesus referred to the earthquakes that will precede His return (Matt. 24:7).

(2) The angel (v. 2*b*)

"For an angel of the Lord descended from heaven."

What caused the earthquake? Most people conclude that Christ's resurrection did. But Matthew tells us that the earthquake occurred because "an angel of the Lord descended from heaven." When the angel touched down on the garden, it created seismic shock waves. The Greek word translated "earthquake" is *seismos*, from which we derive the English word *seismograph*. No doubt the women felt the earthquake as they approached the tomb.

b) The role of the angel (vv. 2*c*-3)

(1) To move the stone (v. 2*c*)

"[He] came and rolled back the stone from the door."

Notice that Matthew doesn't say that the angel let Jesus out of the tomb. Since Jesus had the power to raise Himself from the dead, He certainly didn't have to wait in the tomb until an angel moved the stone to let Him out! No one actually saw the resurrection take place. The women experienced the seismic ramifications of the angel's descent and the other phenomena that accompanied the resurrection. But the resurrection itself was invisible because no one was in the tomb to see it. Christ came out of that grave on His own. The angel didn't move the stone to let the Lord out; he moved it to let the women in so that they could see that Jesus was already gone.

How did Jesus get out of the tomb? In the same way He entered the room where the disciples were meeting eight days later: "Then came Jesus, the door being shut, and stood in the midst" (John 20:26). The same way He came through a wall into the upper room is the same way He passed through the rock of His grave. It wasn't a problem for Him, for He was in His glorified form.

And the angel opened the door to the grave not just to let the women in, but to allow the whole world to see that Jesus wasn't there. When the

50

women arrived, they went in and saw He wasn't there (Luke 24:3). When Peter and John arrived, they went in and saw the linen wrappings undisturbed and the head napkin in a separate place (John 20:6-7). There was no turmoil—no evidence that someone hurriedly unwrapped the body and threw the wrappings on the floor. The wrappings lay just as they had been wrapped about Christ's body—only His body was gone.

(2) To attest to the resurrection (v. 2d)

"[He] sat upon it."

After the angel moved the stone, he sat on it to act as the heavenly witness to what had happened. You can imagine that the Jewish leaders felt secure in the supposition that Jesus was dead and buried, His body held captive in a tomb. But little did they know that all their efforts only served to validate His resurrection.

As the women arrived in the garden, they saw that the tomb was open and the stone rolled back. At this point we need to look at John's gospel to see how Mary Magdalene responded to what she saw. We can't be dogmatic, but it seems that John's narrative fits best in this chronology. John 20:1-2 says, "The first day of the week cometh Mary Magdalene early, when it was yet dark, unto the sepulcher, and seeth the stone taken away from the sepulcher. Then she runneth, and cometh to Simon Peter, and to the other disciple, whom Jesus loved [John], and saith unto them, They have taken away the Lord out of the sepulcher, and we know not where they have laid him." All Mary saw was that the grave was open. She apparently didn't notice the angel.

As we return to Matthew's narrative, Mary Magdalene left to tell Peter and John that the body had been stolen. The other women remained and had the wonderful experience of encountering an angel.

(3) To represent God (v. 3)

"His countenance was like lightning, and his raiment white as snow."

That his face was like lightning represents the essence, the deity, and the brilliance of the character of God. You might compare it to the Shekinah of God as it was transmitted to Moses, whose face radiated the glory of God (Ex. 34:29-35). Matthew also says the angel's garment was white as snow, which represents God's purity and holiness. This holy angel bore the imprimatur of God. He is described in a way that distinguishes him from a man or a demon. He is identified as the agent of God and was a living witness to the risen Christ.

c) The reaction to the angel (v. 4)

"For fear of him the keepers did shake, and became as dead men."

Matthew used the same Greek root for "shake" as he did for "earthquake" in verse 2. So the earth quaked and the guards "shaked"! They not only shook but also became as dead men. They lapsed into a temporary coma out of sheer terror. Fear can paralyze people to the point where they become unconscious. The guards saw something they were unable to comprehend. The women also were afraid, but they were sustained by the angel.

2. The angel's explanation (vv. 5-6b)

a) Offered (v. 5a)

"The angel answered and said unto the women."

A better way to translate that is "the angel explained and said." Some things need explaining even when someone isn't asking questions. This situation definitely needed one: Where was Christ and what was the angel doing there?

b) Examined (vv. 5*b*-6*b*)

    (1) He calmed the women's fears (v. 5*b*)

       "Fear not."

       The soldiers had reason to fear when the angel appeared. But those who loved Christ had no reason to fear.

    (2) He knew the women's objective (v. 5*c*)

       "For I know that ye seek Jesus, who was crucified."

       The angel knew why the women had come to the grave. That had to be a comfort to the women. They had come to find a corpse, not to see a resurrection. They had come out of devotion to anoint a dead body. God didn't rebuke them for their weak faith—He was gracious. They loved the Lord Jesus Christ. In spite of their doubt and despair, God recognized their love and responded in grace.

    (3) He confirmed Christ's resurrection (v. 6*a*)

       "He is not here; for he is risen."

       The literal translation of the Greek text is "he was raised." The Greek word indicates that it was a resurrection from the dead. There's no question that Christ had died. That's why at the crucifixion the Roman soldiers, who were experts at death, didn't break His legs. They thrust a spear into His side to be sure He was dead. The women at the tomb, along with Joseph of Arimathea and Nicodemus, had observed Christ's body closely when they wrapped it with spices. They knew He was dead.

       The Greek verb in Matthew 28:6 is an aorist passive, indicating that Jesus was raised. The Bible emphasizes that He was raised by the power of the Father (Rom. 6:4; Gal. 1:1; 1 Peter 1:3). Jesus also was raised by His own power. In John 10:18 He says, "I have power to lay it [My life] down, and I have power to take it again." And Romans 8:11 says He was raised by the power of the Spirit. The entire Trinity is responsible for the resurrection of Jesus Christ.

(4) He recalled Christ's prophecy (v. 6*b*)

"As he said."

The angel reminded the women that Jesus had said that He would rise on the third day.

3. The angel's invitation (v. 6*c*)

"Come, see the place where the Lord lay."

Luke 24:3 says that they went into the tomb. Luke 24:4 and John 20:12 tell us that a second angel accompanied the first angel—one was at the head of the place where the body once lay, and one was at the feet. That beautiful picture is reminiscent of the Ark of the Covenant. On the top of the Ark of the Covenant was the mercy seat, where atonement was made for sin. Angels were positioned on both sides of the mercy seat. In the tomb the angels were positioned on either side of the absent body of Christ—the same body that was offered as the satisfaction for the sins of the world.

4. The angel's command (v. 7)

a) To exhort the disciples (v. 7*a*)

"Go quickly, and tell his disciples that he is risen from the dead."

I might have been tempted not to tell the disciples. After all, they weren't at the tomb. The disciples were vacillating and weak. They had denied and abandoned the Savior. Yet God didn't want them to know a moment's anguish or misery. He wanted the women to tell them as soon as possible that Christ was raised from the dead. So we see God extend His grace to the disciples.

Conclusion

Why were the women the first to see the angel and the risen Christ? First Corinthians 1:27 says that God chooses the weak to confound the strong. It is also true that He rewards the faithful. Since the women had unselfishly served the Lord in the past, they were to be specially rewarded. It has been said that supreme love deserves supreme privilege. But the main point is that they saw the angel and the living Christ because they were there. If anyone else had been at the tomb, they would have seen the angel and Christ too.

It is good to be present when the Lord does wonderful things. The closer you stay to the Lord, the more you are going to enjoy what He is doing. I would rather experience it myself than hear about it from someone. I praise God for people who are where the Lord is working. They are with His people when they gather together to worship Him. They are present when His Word is taught. They are ready to get on their knees before Him. They are using their gifts in the Lord's service. As a result, they experience firsthand the active power of God.

I hope you will be like those women. What you lack in faith, may you make up in devotion. What you lack in understanding, may you make up in loyalty. God will confirm your weakness and turn it into strength because you are faithful and loyal enough to be where He is when He is working.

Focusing on the Facts

1. What are some of the possible reactions to the resurrection of Jesus Christ? Explain each one (see pp. 42-43).

2. To what end does Matthew build his gospel (see p. 44)?
3. What was the topic of the early church's first sermon (see p. 44)?
4. What is the theme of the New Testament epistles (see p. 44)?
5. What makes Matthew's approach to the resurrection unique (see p. 45)?
6. According to Matthew 28:1, how many days had Christ been in the grave (see p. 46)?
7. Name the women who went to visit Jesus' tomb on Sunday morning (see pp. 47-48).
8. Why did the women go to the grave (Mark 16:1; see p. 48)?
9. What does the earthquake in Matthew 28:2 symbolize? Explain (see p. 49).
10. What caused the earthquake (see pp. 49-50)?
11. Why did the angel roll the stone away from the entrance of the tomb (see p. 50)?
12. Describe the reaction of Mary Magdalene upon seeing that the tomb was empty (John 20:1-2; see p. 51).
13. Describe the appearance of the angel. What does his description represent (Matt. 28:3; see p. 52)?
14. How did the guards react when they saw the angel (Matt. 28:4; see p. 52)?
15. According to Matthew 28:5-6, what did the angel tell the women (see pp. 52-54)?
16. Who is responsible for the resurrection of Jesus Christ? Explain (see p. 54).

Pondering the Principles

1. The women who visited the grave of Jesus Christ on the third day came because they were motivated by one thing: their love for Christ. Look up the following verses: Deuteronomy 6:5; 10:12; Psalm 97:10; 1 John 3:17-18; 4:19-21. Based on those verses, what does love for Jesus Christ mean? Give some examples of how you have manifested your love for Jesus Christ. If at times your love for Him has fallen short of what it should be, confess that right now. Ask God to help you manifest your love for Christ by loving others and obeying His Word.

2. Read Philippians 3:10. What did Paul want to know or experience about the resurrection of Jesus Christ? Read John 14:19, Romans 4:25, and Romans 8:11. What do those verses tell us about the effect of the resurrection on our past, present, and future? Ask God to give you the knowledge that Paul sought.

4
The Resurrection of Jesus Christ—Part 2

Outline

Introduction
A. The Declaration of Our Hope
B. The Guarantee of Our Hope
   1. The resurrection of Christ
   2. The argument of Paul

Review
I. The Time of the Resurrection (v. 1a)
II. The Emotions of the Women (vv. 1b-10)
  A. Sympathy (v. 1b)
  B. Terror (vv. 2-7)
    1. The angel's descent (vv. 2-4)
    2. The angel's explanation (vv. 5-6b)
    3. The angel's invitation (v. 6c)
    4. The angel's command (v. 7)
      a) To exhort the disciples (v. 7a)

Lesson
      b) To enlist the disciples (v. 7b)
  C. Joy (v. 8)
    1. Encountering disbelief
    2. Making a discovery
      a) John and Peter
        (1) Their arrival
        (2) Their response
      b) Mary Magdalene
        (1) Mary's arrival
        (2) Christ's disguise

Introduction

The resurrection of Jesus Christ is the heart of the Christian faith. Christianity is a belief—a series of truths, doctrines, and principles based on the resurrection of Christ. When Jesus rose from the dead by the power of the Father, He proved He was exactly who He claimed to be and that He had accomplished what He came to accomplish. Second Corinthians 4:14 says "that he [God] who raised up the Lord Jesus shall raise up us also." Our belief in resurrection life is built on the resurrection of Jesus Christ. Because He lives, we shall live also (John 14:19).

A. The Declaration of Our Hope

    Throughout Scripture we see the hope of resurrection. Death is not a dead end; it's a thoroughfare to eternity.

    1. Psalm 49:15—The psalmist wrote, "God will redeem my soul from the power of sheol."

    2. Psalm 73:24—Asaph wrote that God would receive him to glory after he died.

    3. Hosea 6:2—Hosea confidently asserted that God will raise up His people so they might live before Him.

    4. Isaiah 26:19—Isaiah wrote, "Thy dead men shall live, together with my dead body shall they arise. Awake and sing, ye that dwell in the dust."

    5. Daniel 12:2—"Many of those who sleep in the dust of the earth shall awake, some to everlasting life."

6. Job 14:14—Job asked, "If a man die, shall he live again? All the days of my appointed time will I wait, till my change come."

7. Job 19:25-27—Job affirmed, "I know that my redeemer liveth, and that he shall stand at the latter day upon the earth; and though after my skin worms destroy this body, yet in my flesh shall I see God, whom I shall see for myself, and mine eyes shall behold, and not another; though my heart be consumed within me."

B. The Guarantee of Our Hope

1. The resurrection of Christ

The hope of God's people is predicated on the resurrection of Jesus Christ. His resurrection guarantees ours. The apostle Paul said, "Now is Christ risen from the dead and become the first fruits of them that slept" (1 Cor. 15:20). No wonder the resurrection of Jesus Christ is mentioned more than a hundred times in the New Testament.

The resurrection may be denied, despised, and mocked. Only a fool would want to explain away the resurrection of Christ, because in so doing he guarantees his eternal doom. The only hope of eternal salvation—of being with God forever in glory—is the resurrection of Christ. To explain it away damns the human race.

The resurrection of Jesus Christ is the single greatest event in the history of the world. It guarantees the resurrection of every saint, no matter what happens to the body. Anyone who denies the literal bodily resurrection of Jesus Christ is not a Christian because he misses the whole point of Christianity.

2. The argument of Paul

In 1 Corinthians 15 the apostle Paul gives a profound argument for the centrality of the resurrection to the Christian faith.

a) There is no good explanation for the empty tomb if there is no resurrection

In verse 13 Paul says, "If there be no resurrection of the dead, then is Christ not risen." That means we have to explain the disappearance of His body in some other way. We have to explain His undisturbed grave clothes somehow. Perhaps someone took His body. Maybe He never was dead—He awoke in the coolness of the tomb, got up, and walked out. But those explanations don't make any sense, given the facts.

b) Preaching the gospel is useless if there is no resurrection

In verse 14 Paul says, "If Christ be not risen, then is our preaching vain." The gospel says that men are sinners, and sinners need a Savior. Christ is that Savior. He paid the penalty for sin, conquered death, and rose from the grave. If He didn't rise, then He is dead, and His payment for sin was not accepted. He wasn't powerful enough. Preaching the gospel is useless when there is no good news to proclaim.

c) Faith is useless if there is no resurrection

Then Paul said, "Your faith is also vain" (v. 14). He repeats that statement in verse 17: "If Christ be not raised, your faith is vain." It's pointless to believe the gospel if Christ didn't rise from the dead.

d) The apostles were liars if there is no resurrection

In verse 15 Paul says, "We are found false witnesses of God, because we have testified of God that he raised up Christ, whom he raised not up, if so be that the dead rise not." Paul was saying that if Christ didn't rise, all the apostles were liars.

e) The power of sin remains if there is no resurrection

Paul continues in verse 17, "If Christ be not raised, your faith is vain, ye are yet in your sins." If Christ didn't rise, the power of sin remains unbroken. Therefore every man is under the domination of sin, forever damned. The resurrection of Jesus Christ is not some negotiable reality; it is the cornerstone of the Christian faith.

f) The dead in Christ are lost if there is no resurrection

In verse 18 Paul says, "They also who are fallen asleep [died] in Christ are perished."

In verse 19 Paul concludes, "If in this life only we have hope in Christ, we are of all men most miserable." If Christ didn't rise from the dead, Christians are the most pitiful people in the world. But Christ did rise!

Review

I. THE TIME OF THE RESURRECTION (v. 1*a*; see pp. 45-47)

"In the end of the sabbath, as it began to dawn toward the first day of the week."

II. THE EMOTIONS OF THE WOMEN (vv. 1*b*-10)

A. Sympathy (v. 1*b*; see pp. 47-49)

"Mary Magdalene and the other Mary [came] to see the sepulcher."

B. Terror (vv. 2-7)

1. The angel's descent (vv. 2-4; see pp. 49-52)

"Behold, there was a great earthquake; for an angel of the Lord descended from heaven, and came and rolled back the stone from the door, and sat upon it. His countenance was like lightning, and his raiment white as snow; and for fear of him the keepers did shake, and became as dead men."

2. The angel's explanation (vv. 5-6*b*; see pp. 52-54)

"The angel answered and said unto the women, Fear not; for I know that ye seek Jesus, who was crucified. He is not here; for he is risen, as he said."

3. The angel's invitation (v. 6*c*; see p. 54)

"Come, see the place where the Lord lay."

4. The angel's command (v. 7)

   a) To exhort the disciples (v. 7*a*; see pp. 54-55)

   "Go quickly, and tell his disciples that he is risen from the dead."

Lesson

   b) To enlist the disciples (v. 7*b*)

   "Behold, he goeth before you into Galilee. There shall ye see him; lo, I have told you."

   Jesus had said to the disciples earlier, "After I am raised up again, I will go before you into Galilee" (Matt. 26:32). Galilee was the region where the Lord first ministered. That also is where He was first hated and rejected.

   In some ways, Galilee was a microcosm of the world. Matthew, quoting Isaiah 9:2, said of it, "The people who sat in darkness saw great light, and to them who sat in the region and shadow of death, light is sprung up" (Matt. 4:16). Christ commissioned the disciples on a mountain in Galilee, saying, "Go therefore and make disciples of all the nations" (Matt. 28:19; NASB). Matthew's gospel ends with that Great Commission—Christ sending out His people with the message of the risen Christ.

Appearances of the Resurrected Christ in Jerusalem

Before meeting the disciples in Galilee, Christ appeared to them and to others in Jerusalem on several occasions.

1. To Mary

On Sunday morning He appeared to Mary Magdalene near the grave. We will see the specifics of that appearance later in our study (see pp. 67-70).

2. To Peter

Later on that same day Christ appeared personally to Peter (Luke 24:34; 1 Cor. 15:5). The Lord was showing grace to one who so pointedly denied Him.

3. To two disciples

Later that afternoon Christ appeared to two disciples traveling to Emmaus. As they walked, the Lord joined them, teaching them what Scripture prophesied about Himself. Later He revealed Himself to them while they ate together (Luke 24:13-32).

4. To the ten disciples

On Sunday night, the disciples were gathered in a room when the Lord appeared to them. Luke 24:36 says, "As they thus spoke, Jesus himself stood in the midst of them, and saith unto them, Peace be unto you. But they were terrified and frightened, and supposed that they had seen a spirit."

5. To Thomas

Since Thomas wasn't with the disciples that first Sunday night, eight days later Jesus appeared again, only this time Thomas was there (John 20:26-27). When Thomas saw Him he said, "My Lord and my God" (v. 28).

Prior to His ascension Christ appeared to His disciples numerous times. Acts 1:3 tells us that Christ "showed himself alive after his passion by many infallible proofs, being seen by them [the apostles] forty days, and speaking of the things pertaining to the kingdom of God." But of all Christ's appearances, the most crucial was His appearance on the mountain in Galilee.

C. Joy (v. 8)

"[The women] departed quickly from the sepulcher with fear and great joy, and did run to bring his disciples word."

The Greek word translated "did run" is the main verb. The angel said "Go!" and they did, running into the city to find the disciples and tell them that Jesus was raised from the dead.

1. Encountering disbelief

When the women found the apostles and delivered their message, the apostles didn't believe them (Mark 16:13). That confirms that the disciples didn't steal Christ's body—they didn't even believe the resurrection had occurred (cf. Luke 24:10-11, 22-25)!

2. Making a discovery

When Mary Magdalene told Peter and John about the empty tomb, they followed her to the sepulcher.

a) John and Peter

(1) Their arrival

John 20:4-5 says, "They [Peter and John] ran both together; and the other disciple [John] did outrun Peter, and came first to the sepulcher. And he, stooping down and looking in, saw the linen clothes lying; yet went he not in."

Verses 6-7 say, "Then cometh Simon Peter following him, and went into the sepulcher, and seeth the linen clothes lying there, and the cloth, that was about his head, not lying with the linen clothes, but wrapped together in a place by itself." That indicates there had been no struggle; Christ simply arose and left the tomb.

(2) Their response

Verse 8 says, "Then went in also that other disciple, who came first to the sepulcher, and he saw, and believed." John had a heart of faith. He quickly moved from curiosity to faith. Verse 9 says, "For as yet they knew not the scripture, that he must rise again from the dead." They had heard Jesus tell them about His resurrection, but they didn't understand it. They were unwilling for Him to die, so they eliminated from their minds the need for Him to rise again.

Verse 10 says, "Then the disciples went away again to their own home." They went away to try to determine what happened. They didn't appear to make any serious investigation about the disappearance of Christ's body.

b) Mary Magdalene

(1) Mary's arrival

But Mary didn't leave; she was ever the devoted follower. Verses 11-14 say, "Mary stood outside of the sepulcher weeping; and as she wept, she stooped down, and looked into the sepulcher, and seeth two angels in white sitting, the one at the head, and the other at the feet, where the body of Jesus had lain. And they say unto her, Woman, why weepest thou? She saith unto them, Because they have taken away my Lord, and I know not where they have laid him. And when she had thus said, she turned herself back."

Mary doesn't appear to have been startled by the presence of the angels. Apparently her sorrow overpowered her ability to realize she was speaking with angels. She responded in a similar manner when she arrived at the tomb earlier. Now she was carrying on a conversation with two angels about the location of Christ's body. Perhaps she assumed that they were men. Scripture is replete with occasions when angels took on the appearance of men (e.g., Gen. 18-19).

(2) Christ's disguise

After turning to leave the tomb, she "saw Jesus standing, and knew not that it was Jesus" (v. 14). Mary was extremely emotional by this time, and it is quite possible that her state of mind prevented her from recognizing Jesus. But it is also the case that after the resurrection no one knew who Jesus was unless He allowed them to. In His resurrection glory He was changed in such a way that He had to reveal Himself to people. How else can we explain the circumstances involving the two disciples who walked and talked with Him, yet didn't know who He was until He disclosed Himself to them (Luke 24:13-32)?

(3) Christ's revelation

Jesus said to Mary, "Woman, why weepest thou? Whom seekest thou? She, supposing him to be the gardener, saith unto him, Sir, if thou have borne him from here, tell me where thou hast laid him, and I will take him away" (John 20:15). Mary may have believed the grave was available for only a few days, and that Jesus' body had been moved. Verse 16 says, "Jesus saith unto her, Mary." Jesus addressed her in Aramaic—her own language—which added a personal touch. Instantly she knew who He was. Verse 16 says, "She turned herself, and saith unto him, Rabboni; which is to say, Master." The title *Rabboni*, a step above Rabbi, was used only for a highly exalted teacher. Mark 16:9 tells us Mary was the first person to see the resurrected Christ.

(4) Christ's command

In John 20:17 Jesus tells Mary, "Touch me not" ("Don't cling to Me"). Jesus said that because Mary grabbed ahold of Him. Mary had lost Jesus once—she wasn't going to lose Him again! The pain of His death and absence was more than she could bear. Then Jesus said, "I am not yet ascended to my Father. But go to my brethren, and say unto them, I ascend unto my Father and your Father, and to my God and your God" (v. 17).

Two things are important to note from that verse. First, before His death Jesus called His disciples friends (John 15:15). But from this point on He would call them brethren. Why? Because His death and resurrection brought them completely into the family of God. Paul said we "are heirs of God and joint heirs with Christ" (Rom. 8:17). Hebrews 2:11 says that Christ "is not ashamed to call them brethren." But most important are the words Christ used to emphasize the new relationship: "I ascend unto my Father and your Father, and to my God and your God." The disciples abandoned Christ to His captors, but in spite of that, He would draw them to Himself. Now they had the same Father, God Himself.

(5) Mary's response

John 20:18 says, "Mary Magdalene came and told the disciples that she had seen the Lord, and that he had spoken these things unto her." She was always willing to help her Lord fulfill His divine agenda.

As we return to Matthew 28, let's establish the scene. The women left the empty tomb to tell the disciples. Mary Magdalene returned to the grave, and Peter and John followed. After Peter and John went into the tomb, they returned home. Mary lingered and saw Christ. Now she left to tell the disciples what she saw and heard. While the other women were still on their way to find all the disciples, the Lord supernaturally transported Himself to meet them.

D. Worship (v. 9)

1. Christ's greeting (v. 9a)

"As they went to tell his disciples, behold, Jesus met them, saying, All hail [Gk., *chairete*]."

There was Christ in His resurrection glory, but what did He say? "Hi!" He greeted them with the normal greeting of the day. It was how people greeted each other as they passed along the roads. In a simple and warm way Jesus stopped the women and greeted them. Although Jesus was glorified, He had not lost His human tenderness. He communes with holy angels and the Trinity, but He also communes with men and women who walk the dusty roads of life.

2. The women's gratitude (v. 9b)

"They came and held him by the feet, and worshiped him."

They knew He was the risen Christ, so they worshiped Him. He was to be adored, praised, glorified, and honored. They did what Paul says everyone should do: "At the name of Jesus every knee should bow . . . and that every tongue should confess that Jesus Christ is Lord, to the glory of God, the Father" (Phil. 2:10-11). They paid Him homage as God.

When I look at the cross I feel pain. When I study the resurrection, and the earthquake that revealed the empty tomb, I'm filled with terror and the fear of almighty power. Then I become alert and alive to the resurrection, and my heart is filled with joy in seeing the risen Christ. Then I fall at the Savior's feet in worship.

Evidence for the Resurrection

Evidence for the resurrection is abundantly available. The women were immediate eyewitnesses of the evidence that the resurrection took place: the broken seal, the empty tomb, the grave clothes, the unconscious soldiers, and the testimony of the angels. But when they touched the risen Lord, they knew He was not a figment of their imaginations. They held Him by His feet.

Sir Edward Clarke said, "As a lawyer I have made a prolonged study of the evidences for the events of the first Easter Day. To me the evidence is conclusive, and over and over again in the High Court I have secured the verdict on evidence not nearly so compelling. Inference follows on evidence, and a truthful witness is always artless and disdains effect. The Gospel evidence for the resurrection is of this class, and as a lawyer I accept it unreservedly as the testimony of truthful men to facts they were able to substantiate" (see below for documentation).

Professor Thomas Arnold, author of the three-volume *History of Rome* and an appointee to the chair of modern history at Oxford University, wrote, "The evidence for our Lord's life and death and resurrection may be, and often has been, shown to be satisfactory; it is good according to the common rules for distinguishing good evidence from bad. Thousands and tens of thousands of persons have gone through it piece by piece as carefully as every judge summing up on a most important case. I have myself done it many times over, not to persuade others but to satisfy myself. I have been used for many years to study the histories of other times, and to examine and weigh the evidence of those who have written about them, and I know of no one fact in the history of mankind which is proved by better and fuller evidence of every sort, to the understanding of a fair inquirer, than the great sign which God hath given us that Christ died and rose again from the dead." (For documentation and attestation from other experts see Josh McDowell's *Evidence That Demands a Verdict* [San Bernardino, Calif.: Here's Life, 1979], pp. 179-263.)

E. Hope (v. 10)

"Then said Jesus unto them, Be not afraid; go tell my brethren that they go into Galilee, and there shall they see me."

Their hope was clear. The risen Christ would again manifest Himself. Jesus repeated the same message the angel gave them, thus showing us the source of the angelic message.

Conclusion

Matthew's treatment of the resurrection is simple and unpretentious. It's not something he worked hard at trying to prove. Matthew stated the simple, convincing truth. Before Christ's time on earth came to an end, He appeared to His people so that they might confirm His resurrection. From them He selected the ones who would write the New Testament—the record of His resurrection and the meaning of it.

What Does the Resurrection Prove?

1. That the Bible is the Word of God

   Over and over again Jesus said He would rise in three days, and He did. The resurrection affirms that the record of Scripture is true.

2. That Jesus Christ is the Son of God

   Christ claimed to be the Son of God and to have power over death. His resurrection proves He did.

3. That salvation is complete

   Christ conquered sin, death, and hell on the cross, and He rose victorious to prove that He did.

4. That the church was established

   In Matthew 16:18 Jesus says, "I will build my church, and the gates of hades shall not prevail against it." The phrase "gates of hades" was a colloquial expression for death. Death couldn't stop Christ from building His church, and His resurrection proved it.

5. That judgment is coming

In John 5:27 Jesus says that the Father has "given him authority to execute judgment." He has the power to raise the dead and judge them. Some will enter eternal life and some will experience eternal judgment (vv. 28-29). The Judge is alive, and one day His court will be in session to determine the eternal destiny of every man and woman.

6. That heaven is waiting

In John 14:2 Jesus says, "In my Father's house are many mansions. . . . I go to prepare a place for you." Heaven is waiting; the risen Christ is even now preparing it for His own.

The resurrection proves it all. I trust that you not only believe in the resurrection but also have received Jesus Christ as your Lord and Savior, for the one should naturally lead to the other.

Focusing on the Facts

1. What does Scripture teach about the believer's hope (see pp. 60-61)?
2. What guarantees the believer's resurrection (see p. 61)?
3. To show the centrality of the resurrection to the Christian faith, Paul presents a classic argument in 1 Corinthians 15. Explain the various statements Paul makes in the course of his argument (see pp. 61-63).
4. How did Paul conclude his argument (1 Cor. 15:19; see p. 63)?
5. Where was Christ planning to commission His disciples to take the gospel to the world (Matt. 28:7; see p. 64)?
6. To whom did Christ appear in Jerusalem after He was raised (see p. 65)?
7. What kind of reception did the women receive when they told the disciples what the angel said (Mark 16:13; see p. 66)?
8. Describe the reactions of John and Peter when they examined the empty tomb (John 20:4-10; see pp. 66-67).
9. What did Mary Magdalene do after Peter and John left the tomb (John 20:11-14; see p. 67)?
10. Why was Mary unable to recognize Jesus at first (see p. 68)?
11. When did Mary recognize Jesus (John 20:16; see p. 68)?

12. Why did Christ refer to His disciples as brethren after His resurrection (see p. 69)?
13. How did the other women respond when Christ personally revealed Himself to them (Matt. 28:9; see p. 70)?
14. What does the resurrection prove? Explain (see pp. 72-73).

Pondering the Principles

1. Reread the section on the declaration of our hope (see pp. 60-61). It surveys what the Old Testament says about life after death. As you read through and study the New Testament, make a list of verses that refer to the believer's hope. As your list expands, you will have a definitive record of what Scripture teaches on that subject. You also will have a source of great comfort when you are besieged with the trials of life.

2. When the risen Christ appeared before the women, they worshiped Him. Read Philippians 2:5-11. Why is Jesus Christ worthy of worship? Why did God exalt Him? Who should worship Christ? Verse 5 tells us to have the same attitude Christ did. Verses 1-4 spell out that attitude. Does your life-style reveal that you daily confess Jesus Christ as Lord? Don't be just a hearer of God's Word; be a doer (James 1:22). Be open about your love for Jesus Christ, just as the women were who fell at His feet.

5

The Lie That Proves the Resurrection

Outline

Introduction
A. Rejecting the Resurrection
B. Explaining the Resurrection
  1. The swoon theory
     a) Discussed
     b) Disproved
        (1) The testimony of the witnesses
           (*a*) The preparers
           (*b*) The soldiers
        (2) The severity of the injuries
  2. The no-burial theory
     a) Discussed
     b) Disproved
  3. The hallucination theory
     a) Discussed
     b) Disproved
  4. The telepathy theory
     a) Discussed
     b) Disproved
  5. The seance theory
     a) Discussed
     b) Disproved
  6. The mistaken-identity theory
     a) Discussed
     b) Disproved
  7. The deluded-woman theory
  8. The theft theory

Lesson
I. The Plot (vv. 11-15a)
   A. The Report of the Soldiers (v. 11)
      1. Their decision
      2. Their duty
      3. Their description
   B. The Reaction of the Leaders (vv. 12-14)
      1. Convening the Sanhedrin (v. 12a)
      2. Passing a resolution (vv. 12b-14)
         a) Its purpose (v. 12b)
         b) Its essence (vv. 12c-14)
            (1) Bribery (v. 12c)
            (2) Deception (v. 13)
            (3) Protection (v. 14)
   C. The Response of the Soldiers (v. 15a)
II. The Propagation (v. 15b)
   A. Proof of the Resurrection from Christ's Friends
      1. Their unanimity
      2. Their transformation
   B. Proof of the Resurrection from Christ's Enemies
      1. The importance of their explanation
      2. The impossibility of their explanation
         a) The cowardice of the disciples
            (1) They didn't have the means to bribe the soldiers
            (2) They couldn't sneak past the soldiers
            (3) They didn't anticipate a resurrection
         b) The training of the soldiers
         c) The bribery from the leaders
         d) The lie of the soldiers

Conclusion

Introduction

Matthew 28:11-15 says, "Behold, some of the watch [Roman guard] came into the city, and showed unto the chief priests all the things that were done. And when they were assembled with the elders, and had taken counsel, they gave much money unto the soldiers, saying, Say ye, His disciples came by night, and stole him away while we slept. And if this come to the governor's ears, we will persuade him, and secure you. So they took the money, and did as they were taught; and this saying is commonly reported among the

Jews until this day." That narrative describes bribery and the perpetration of a lie about the resurrection of Jesus Christ.

G. B. Hardy wrote a book about destiny (*Countdown: A Time to Choose* [Chicago: Moody, 1971]). In it he asked two important questions: "Has anyone cheated death and proved it?" and, "Is it available to me?" (p. 32). He found the answers to his questions in the resurrection of Jesus Christ.

A. Rejecting the Resurrection

Jesus Christ defeated death, and He made a way for you and me to defeat it as well. There is no hope of heaven, of eternal blessing and joy, without the resurrection of Christ. But in spite of that, most people reject it. To do so, for whatever reason, is to commit spiritual suicide. Such people forfeit all hope of a future in heaven. Their souls are damned to an eternal hell without God. Not only do they lose future blessing, but also the meaning and value of the present. If the future holds no meaning, how can the present have any meaning?

To deny the hope of eternal life is to oppose humanity's innate desire for immortality. Ecclesiastes 3:11 says that God has set eternity in the heart of every man and woman. Something inside man reaches out for immortality—he is not satisfied with life on a temporal level only. The myriad religions and philosophies throughout history reflect that desire. The resurrection of Jesus Christ is the key to that desire. Jesus said, "Because I live, ye shall live also" (John 14:19). He also said, "I am the resurrection, and the life; he that believeth in me, though he were dead, yet shall he live. And whosoever liveth and believeth in me shall never die" (John 11:25-26). The Bible tells us that if Christ did not rise, no one has any hope. But He did, so we have hope for eternal life (1 Cor. 15:17-20). Yet men continue to reject that hope.

B. Explaining the Resurrection

Throughout the years many theories have been proposed to explain away the truth of the resurrection. Let me relate some of them.

1. The swoon theory

a) Discussed

Those who hold to the swoon theory believe that Christ never died. They claim He went into a coma because of shock from a great loss of blood and the trauma His body endured on the cross. When He was removed from the cross and laid in the tomb, the aroma of the spices and the coolness of the tomb supposedly revived Him. It is then asserted that He somehow came out of the grave, fooling the disciples into believing He had been resurrected.

b) Disproved

(1) The testimony of the witnesses

(a) The preparers

All the early records are emphatic in stating that Jesus had died. The women, Joseph of Arimathea, and Nicodemus must have known whether He was dead when they carefully wrapped His body in linen and anointed Him. They certainly would have noticed any sign of life, considering the care with which they handled His body.

(b) The soldiers

The Romans were expert executioners—they knew when someone was dead. They didn't break Jesus' legs because it was obvious that He was already dead. When they rammed a spear into His side and blood and water came out, they knew for certain that He was dead.

(2) The severity of the injuries

If the swoon theory is to be believed, Jesus would have had to survive a severe beating and a loss of blood, a crucifixion with further loss of blood, and a mortal spear wound in His side. He would have had to survive entombment with over seventy pounds of spices packed about His already weakened body. He would have had to survive three days without food or water. Then He would have had to wake up in the dark tomb and without medical assistance, move the stone, and walk out of the tomb. Once He was outside, He would have had to overpower the entire Roman guard, and then walk seven miles to Emmaus on feet that had been pierced with nails!

2. The no-burial theory

   a) Discussed

   Those who believe the no-burial theory claim that Christ was never put in the tomb. They argue instead that Christ's body was thrown into a pit with the bodies of other criminals. Christ's followers, however, believed He was put in the tomb, and when He wasn't there on Sunday, they believed He had been raised.

   b) Disproved

   No evidence exists to support the view that any of the activities described by the no-burial advocates ever took place. Why would the Jewish leaders seal the tomb and post a Roman guard if Christ's body had been thrown in a pit? They could have disproved the resurrection simply by retrieving His body from the pit and producing it as evidence.

3. The hallucination theory

   a) Discussed

   Those who support the hallucination theory say that Christ's followers only thought they saw Jesus, because they wanted to see Him so badly. They argue that the disciples were so excited in their anticipation of the resurrection that they experienced a hallucination.

b) Disproved

How could five hundred people (1 Cor. 15:6) have had the same hallucination at the same time? Since Christ's closest followers didn't expect a resurrection, where did they acquire a desire for a resurrection so strong that it caused them to hallucinate? And the question still remains: Even if they did hallucinate, what happened to Christ's body?

4. The telepathy theory

a) Discussed

Some have suggested that there was no physical resurrection, but that instead God sent mental images into the minds of Christ's followers.

b) Disproved

This theory makes God a deceiver and the apostles liars. If the theory were true, the two disciples going from Jerusalem to Emmaus carried on a conversation with an image even as they walked seven miles over dusty roads—an unlikely event. Later they ate with that same image. However, Christianity is not founded on deception.

5. The seance theory

a) Discussed

The seance theory states that some medium conjured up the spirit of the dead Jesus through occult power.

b) Disproved

How could Christ's followers have touched Him and held His feet if He were a spirit? In Luke 24:39 Jesus says, "Handle me, and see; for a spirit hath not flesh and bones, as ye see me have." How could Jesus have eaten if He were a spirit (cf. Luke 24:40-43)? And once again, where was His body? Why was the tomb empty if Jesus' appearances were nothing more than some projection by a medium?

6. The mistaken-identity theory

   a) Discussed

   Some claim that someone impersonated Jesus as a way of accomplishing a fake resurrection.

   b) Disproved

   If we assume that assertion, the impostor must have crucified himself to produce the wounds in his hands and feet, and stabbed himself to produce his punctured side. However, that's an unreasonably high price to pay for faking something. How can you explain the post-resurrection miracles if he were an impostor? How can you explain his walking through walls, routing the fish in the Sea of Galilee to the disciples' net, appearing and vanishing at will, and ascending into heaven in full view of the apostles? No impersonator can do that. Besides, the disciples knew Jesus too well to be fooled. And then again we ask, where was the body?

7. The deluded-woman theory

   The nineteenth-century French scholar Ernest Renan attempted to debunk the resurrection of Jesus Christ by claiming it was based on the testimony of an eccentric, delirious, frightened woman named Mary Magdalene. He implied that since she had been possessed by seven demons (Luke 8:2), she merely imagined that she saw the resurrected Christ (*The Life of Jesus* [New York: Carleton, 1886], p. 357).

   But Renan must have forgotten that there were more than five hundred witnesses. He must have forgotten the ten separate appearances of Christ recorded in the gospels (see p. 87). And he doesn't explain what happened to the body of Christ. If the Jewish leaders had produced His body, they would have stopped all apostolic preaching of the resurrection. Any theory that denies the resurrection must explain what happened to the body.

8. The theft theory

The theory that the disciples stole Christ's body was adopted by the Jewish leaders (Matt. 28:11-15). This is the only theory that makes any sense because it's the only one that attempts to deal with the absence of Christ's body. The Jewish leaders wouldn't have taken the body because they had no reason to fake a resurrection. The Romans wouldn't have taken it because they weren't interested. Only the friends of Jesus had a reason for stealing Christ's body.

Matthew concluded his narrative on the resurrection of Christ with the lie perpetrated by the Jewish leaders. Why did Matthew decide to end on a negative note? Why didn't he conclude his account like John did, giving us testimony of the witnesses affirming the resurrection? He did so for two reasons. First, he wanted to demonstrate that the apostasy of the Jewish leaders was final. They denied the resurrection, just as they had denied everything else about Jesus Christ. Second, the testimony of Christ's enemies is the best testimony to the reality of His resurrection. We would expect His followers to attest to His resurrection, but not His enemies. And this unexpected incident involving His enemies is a marked and significant proof of the resurrection. The narrative itself is a compelling apologetic.

Lesson

I. THE PLOT (vv. 11-15*a*)

As we approach the text, we need to remember the context (see pp. 45-55; 63-72). It was now Sunday morning—the third day since Jesus had been placed in the tomb. As a group of women approached the tomb, an earthquake occurred. When they arrived, they discovered that the stone covering the entrance of the tomb had been rolled away. Sitting on the stone was an angel clothed in white garments and sent from God. His descent from heaven was the cause of the earthquake. The angel announced to the women that Christ was no longer in the grave—that He was alive. They looked in the tomb and discovered he was right. Then they left to inform the disciples. While they were walking along the road, the risen Christ met them and spoke to them.

Matthew 28:4 tells us what happened to the Roman soldiers when they saw the angel: "For fear of him the keepers did shake, and became as dead men." They felt the earthquake and saw the stone moved away. Then they saw the angel, and their fear of him caused them to faint.

A. The Report of the Soldiers (v. 11)

"Now when they [the women] were going, behold, some of the watch came into the city, and showed unto the chief priests all the things that were done."

1. Their decision

In verse 10 the risen Christ says to the women, "Be not afraid; go tell my brethren that they go into Galilee, and there shall they see me." As the women were going to find the disciples, some of the guard came into the city. We don't know precisely when the guard came out of their coma and went into the city, but it was around the time the women went to fulfill Christ's command.

Matthew said that some—not all—of the guard went into the city to report what happened to the chief priests. Perhaps as many as a dozen went, while some remained by the grave. It might be that some of them were too frightened to admit they had lost the body they were supposed to be guarding. They were aware of the Roman law stating that if a soldier failed in his duty, he paid with his life.

2. Their duty

The soldiers had a duty to report back to the chief priests. They didn't report to Pilate because he had given the chief priests authority over them. Matthew 27:62-66 reminds us that "the chief priests and Pharisees came together unto Pilate, saying, Sir, we remember that that deceiver said, while he was yet alive, After three days I

83

will rise again. Command, therefore, that the sepulcher be made sure until the third day, lest his disciples come by night, and steal him away, and say unto the people, He is risen from the dead; so the last error shall be worse than the first. Pilate said unto them, Ye have a watch; go your way, make it as sure as ye can. So they went, and made the sepulcher sure, sealing the stone, and setting a watch." At that time the Jewish leaders took charge of the soldiers and set the guard. They would have warned the guard because Christ claimed He would rise on the third day, and the disciples might try to steal the body. So the guard would have been alert, anticipating an appearance by the disciples.

3. Their description

Matthew 28:11 says that the guard "showed unto the chief priests all the things that were done." That means they told them about the earthquake, about the stone being rolled away, and about the arrival of the angel.

I believe the Jewish leaders were the first to hear secondhand about the resurrection—even before the disciples. But they didn't believe. Two days previous they had mockingly said, "Let him now come down from the cross, and we will believe him" (Matt. 27:42). And here was something greater—He had come out of the grave. But they didn't believe; they didn't even investigate the soldiers' story. They were so resistant, so blind, so sinful, and so locked within their own religious system that they would not investigate the report. They refused to believe. Second Corinthians 4:4 tells us why: "The god of this age [Satan] hath blinded the minds of them who believe not." The news brought shock and fear, but it did not bring repentance and faith. The religious leaders were without excuse. They were informed about the resurrection, yet they didn't bother to investigate its validity. They did do one thing—determine a way to prevent others from hearing about it.

B. The Reaction of the Leaders (vv. 12-14)

1. Convening the Sanhedrin (v. 12*a*)

"When they were assembled with the elders."

That phrase is used frequently in Matthew to refer to an official meeting of the Sanhedrin, the ruling body of elders in Israel. They convened immediately to deal with the supernatural events that had occurred at the grave of Christ. The leaders realized that if they allowed the people to believe that Jesus was alive, they would have a worse situation on their hands than ever before (Matt. 27:64). They feared the whole nation would follow Christ. So they decided to lie about the resurrection.

2. Passing a resolution (vv. 12*b*-14)

   a) Its purpose (v. 12*b*)

   "Had taken counsel."

   That phrase (used in Matt. 12:14; 22:15; 27:1, 7) refers to making a formal resolution. At this official convening of the Sanhedrin, the elders passed a formal resolution regarding how they would handle the disappearance of Jesus' body from the tomb.

   b) Its essence (vv. 12*c*-14)

   (1) Bribery (v. 12*c*)

   "They gave much money [Gk., *arguria*, "silver money"] unto the soldiers."

   The rulers bought off Judas Iscariot for thirty pieces of silver, but they had to pay much more to the soldiers. After all, there may have been a dozen of them. And they might have given more than thirty pieces of silver per soldier. But it didn't matter—the leaders were willing to pay any price to perpetrate their lie about the resurrection. What they could not afford was allowing the people to believe that Jesus had risen from the dead.

(2) Deception (v. 13)

"Say ye, His disciples came by night, and stole him away while we slept."

The soldiers knew that wasn't the truth—that's not what they reported. But the Jewish leaders bribed them to lie about the resurrection. Since the grave was empty, the only theory that made sense was that the disciples stole the body.

(3) Protection (v. 14)

"If this [the story that the soldiers were sleeping when the disciples stole the body] come to the governor's [Pilate's] ears, we will persuade him, and secure you."

The Greek phrase translated "persuade him, and secure you" literally means, "satisfy him and make you without anxiety." The soldiers were afraid that if Pilate heard that the body was stolen while they slept, they would be court-martialed and executed. So the Sanhedrin assured the soldiers that they would take care of things if Pilate found out. By now they were experts at coercing the cowardly governor.

So that was the resolution voted on and passed in the Sanhedrin. Therein lies Matthew's final testimony to the apostasy of Israel's leaders. The greatest miracle Jesus ever performed was His own resurrection from the dead, yet the rulers were interested only in denying it.

C. The Response of the Soldiers (v. 15a)

"So they took the money, and did as they were taught."

The soldiers did as they had been instructed: they proclaimed the lie. Even to this day the prevalent theory against the resurrection is the "theft theory."

II. THE PROPAGATION (v. 15b)

"This saying [Gk., *logos*] is commonly reported among the Jews until this day."

Matthew wrote his gospel probably around A.D. 63. So thirty years later the theory that the disciples stole Christ's body was continuing to circulate among the Jewish people. The soldiers knew the truth. They had been at the tomb and experienced the phenomena of the resurrection to some degree, yet they were not believers. To the contrary, they became preachers of an anti-gospel. And their lie still exists today.

The narrative regarding the lie concludes in Matthew 28:15. But if we stop there we will miss Matthew's reason for including it. The lie perpetrated by the Jewish leaders supplies convincing proof of the reality of the resurrection. It accomplishes the opposite of what it was intended to accomplish. Most importantly, it is evidence given not by Jesus' friends, but by His enemies.

A. Proof of the Resurrection from Christ's Friends

1. Their unanimity

Matthew, Mark, Luke, and John all tell us about the physical resurrection of Christ. Their testimony includes the following facts: the stone was moved, Christ's grave clothes remained in perfect order, there was an earthquake, holy angels gave testimony about the reality of the resurrection, and there were ten separate appearances of Jesus after His resurrection. He appeared (1) to Mary Magdalene (John 20:14), (2) to the other women (Matt. 28:9), (3) to Peter (Luke 24:34; 1 Cor. 15:5), (4) to the two disciples on the road to Emmaus (Luke 24:13-32), (5) to ten of the disciples in the upper room (John 20:19-24), (6) to the eleven disciples, including Thomas, eight days later (John 20:26-29), (7) to seven disciples in Galilee (John 21), (8) to the five hundred (1 Cor. 15:6), (9) to James (1 Cor. 15:7), and (10) to the eleven on the Mount of Olives as He ascended into heaven (Acts 1:1-9). Now that's convincing testimony—so much so that

Acts 1:3 says, "He showed himself alive after his passion by many infallible proofs." It is even more convincing when we realize that at one time the disciples didn't expect there would be a resurrection. However, they were soon convinced and were unanimous and unwavering in their testimony.

2. Their transformation

Luke 24:11 says that when the women reported to the disciples that Jesus was alive, "their words seemed to them as idle tales." John 20:9 says, "As yet they knew not the scripture, that he must rise again from the dead." They weren't anticipating a resurrection. What transformed the disciples, who didn't expect a resurrection, from being the cowardly, spiritually dull pessimists that they were into heroes who fully believed in it? How could this group of men, who ran in fear from the Jewish leaders when Jesus was taken captive, run in courage to the same leaders and proclaim the resurrection? When the religious leaders told them to stop, Peter said, "We cannot but speak the things which we have seen and heard" (Acts 4:20). On another occasion he said, "We must obey God rather than men!" (Acts 5:29, NIV*). So what changed them? Prior to the resurrection Peter ran in fear denying his association with Jesus. Then on the Day of Pentecost he preached the gospel before thousands of people, indicting them for crucifying and killing their Lord (Acts 2:23; 3:14-15).

By what power were they transformed? It wasn't the power of their speech. They were not trained orators and masters of eloquence and logic. What made the difference in their lives? The reality of the resurrection (Acts 4:13). They believed it because of the evidence. They had a compelling, powerful faith that caused them to die for the truth of the resurrection.

B. Proof of the Resurrection from Christ's Enemies

New International Version.

1. The importance of their explanation

   It was impossible for the Jewish leaders and Roman soldiers to deny that Christ left the grave by supernatural means. They saw the evidence. If His body were still in the grave, they would have produced it and thereby have proven that the resurrection was a hoax. But the tomb was empty. The earthquake and the angel proved something supernatural had occurred. To deny the resurrection, they had no other choice but to claim that someone took Christ's body.

2. The impossibility of their explanation

   a) The cowardice of the disciples

   Before the resurrection, the disciples acted like cowards. Shortly before Christ was arrested in the Garden of Gethsemane, He predicted that all the disciples would forsake Him and flee (Matt. 26:31). The Old Testament prophets predicted it as well (Zech. 13:7). When the entourage of chief priests, religious dignitaries, and Roman soldiers went into the garden, they found Christ with His disciples (John 18:2-4). As the Lord spoke His name, everyone in the mob was knocked flat on his back (v. 6). At that point the disciples felt invincible. Peter drew his sword and was prepared to fight (v. 10). He felt secure after what the Lord had just done to the mob. After Peter cut off the ear of the high priest's slave, Christ commanded him to put his sword away (v. 11). Jesus then healed the slave's ear (Luke 22:51) and allowed Himself to be taken captive (John 18:12). As soon as Christ was taken, the disciples panicked and ran (Matt. 26:56). They were afraid. They didn't want to confront the mob—they knew they could lose their lives. Later, while in the courtyard of the high priest, Peter was confronted about his association with Christ. He denied following Christ or even knowing Him (Matt. 26:69-75).

   If the disciples stole the body, how did they acquire the courage to pursue their plan, once they saw the

Roman guard at the tomb? These same men did not remain alongside the living Christ when He was taken captive, even after seeing His power on display. How can we believe they would take a stand apart from the comforting presence of Christ against the same people they ran from earlier? We can't! They were hiding out in fear. Peter, the boldest, strongest, and most courageous of the disciples, denied Jesus Christ verbally before a slave girl (Matt. 26:69)!

(1) They didn't have the means to bribe the soldiers

The disciples couldn't have bribed the soldiers— they didn't have enough money. Matthew 28:12 says the Jewish leaders had to give them *much* money.

(2) They couldn't sneak past the soldiers

Some believe that a few of the disciples distracted the soldiers while the others went in the tomb and took the body. That means they would have had to have been extremely fast. If that were true, then why would they take the time to unwrap all the grave clothes and lay them out carefully in the grave? If speed were an issue, they would have picked up Christ's body and run out of the tomb as fast as they could. And how could they have rolled the stone from the entrance without the soldiers noticing?

(3) They didn't anticipate a resurrection

The disciples didn't anticipate the need for a resurrection, so why would they fake one? Why would they be willing to die for what they knew to be a hoax?

b) The training of the soldiers

It is difficult to believe that all the Roman soldiers would have been asleep, because they knew better. When Roman soldiers stood guard at night, they divided their time into four watches. A watch would last no more than three hours and no less than two. That's not a long period of time for anyone to stay awake, let alone a trained Roman soldier. After a soldier had stood his watch, another soldier took his place while the others slept. Since they rotated the watch, it's highly unlikely that they all fell asleep at the same time. Furthermore, if a Roman soldier fell asleep while he was on guard and thus failed to fulfill his duty, he paid with his life. The price was too high to risk falling asleep.

c) The bribery from the leaders

Another factor that makes the explanation of the Jewish leaders impossible to believe is that they would not have bribed the soldiers to tell the truth. People don't bribe people to tell the truth; they bribe them to lie.

d) The lie of the soldiers

In Matthew 28:13 we read that the Sanhedrin told the soldiers to say, "His disciples came by night, and stole him away while we slept." But how could they have known what had happened while they were asleep? Could they have seen the disciples steal the body while they were sleeping? Of course not. If they were asleep, they would not have known what happened.

Such explanations are an offense to logic and reason.

By recording the lie perpetrated by the Jewish leaders, Matthew showed that any explanation other than the resurrection is absurd. The testimony of Scripture is that Jesus rose from the dead. Both the testimony of Christ's friends and enemies support that conclusion.

Conclusion

Simon Greenleaf, the famous Harvard professor of law, wrote, "All that Christianity asks of men . . . is, that they would be consistent with themselves; that they would treat its evidences as they treat the evidence of other things; and that they would try and judge its actors and witnesses, as they deal with their fellow men, when testifying to human affairs and actions, in human tribunals. . . . The result, it is confidently believed, will be an undoubting conviction of their integrity, ability, and truth" (*Testimony of the Evangelists, Examined by the Rules of Evidence Administered in Courts of Justice* [Grand Rapids: Baker, 1965 reprint], p. 46). The assessment of those who have extensively studied the resurrection is that no other historical event is as thoroughly attested to as the resurrection of Jesus Christ (cf. McDowell, p. 71). The folly of alternate explanations is merely another demonstration of its reality.

Because Jesus lives, He gives life to all who believe in Him. Romans 10:9-10 says, "If thou shalt confess with thy mouth the Lord Jesus, and shalt believe in thine heart that God hath raised him from the dead, thou shalt be saved. For with the heart man believeth unto righteousness; and with the mouth confession is made unto salvation." And salvation is equal to eternal life, deliverance from sin, and hope. Our salvation secures our eternal destiny in the presence of God in the glories of heaven. But it belongs only to those who believe in the resurrection and confess Jesus as Lord, thereby identifying themselves with Him.

How do you respond to the resurrection? Many try to explain it away, and in doing so commit spiritual suicide. They kill their hope for the future and the meaning of life in the present. But many believe because the facts are so clear and the evidence is so strong. May you stand in that company.

Focusing on the Facts

1. In a sense, what are people doing when they reject the truth of the resurrection of Jesus Christ? Explain (see p. 77).
2. What is the only thing that will fulfill man's innate desire for immortality (see p. 77)?
3. Name the different theories that have been proposed to explain away the resurrection. Explain each one (see pp. 77-82).
4. What must any theory that denies the resurrection explain (see p. 82)?
5. Why did Matthew conclude his treatment of the resurrection with the lie perpetrated by the Jewish leaders (see p. 82)?

6. How many soldiers left Christ's tomb and went into the city (see p. 83)?
7. To whom did the guard report? Why (Matt. 27:62-66; see pp. 83-84)?
8. How did the Jewish leaders respond when confronted with the report of the soldiers (see pp. 84-85)?
9. What did the Sanhedrin decide to do about the soldiers' report? Explain (Matt. 28:12-14; see pp. 85-86).
10. How did the soldiers respond to the decision of the Sanhedrin (Matt. 28:15; see p. 86)?
11. Cite the ten separate appearances of the resurrected Christ as recorded in Scripture (see p. 87).
12. Describe the changes in Peter following the resurrection and ascension of Christ (see p. 88).
13. Describe the behavior of the disciples at the time Jesus was taken captive in the Garden of Gethsemane (see p. 89)?
14. Why couldn't the disciples have stolen Christ's body (see p. 90)?
15. How can we be confident that not all of the Roman soldiers would have fallen asleep (see pp. 90-91)?
16. How do we know that what the leaders told the soldiers to say was an obvious lie (see p. 91)?

Pondering the Principles

1. Read 1 Corinthians 15:12-57. List all the basic truths of the resurrection that the apostle Paul discusses. Which ones have you been familiar with, and which ones had you forgotten? Meditate on the passages that are most meaningful to you. Then thank the Lord for His plan of salvation, which includes your own bodily resurrection.

2. Use this study to formulate your own apologetic on the resurrection. Record the pertinent details from this chapter to answer the question, How do we know that Jesus rose from the dead? Share your work with your pastor and fellow believers. You'll find their comments and suggestions helpful in fine-tuning your apologetic. When you feel prepared, ask God to bring people into your path who need to know the evidence of the resurrection.

Scripture Index

97

Topical Index

responses to Christ's, 42-43,
70, 77, 92
theories attempting to explain
away Christ's, 38, 61,
77-92
time of Christ's, 45-47
Trinity's role in Christ's, 53-
54
Roman guard, training of, 90-91
Ruth, providence of God and,
31

Sabbath, the
duration of, 9
ending era of, 46-47
killing Lord of, 12
Passover, 11, 34
preparation for, 10-12, 34
Sunday and, 46-47
Sadducees, the
apostasy of, 82
bribery by, 76-77, 82-92

hatred of Christ, 34-39, 83-84
Pharisees and, 34
Salome, mother of James and
John
loyalty of, 47-48, 55
worship by, 70
Service, loyal. *See* Loyalty
Sovereignty of God, the
definition of, 24
doctrine of, 24-25
miracles and, 25-27
personal application of, 39-40
providence and, 27-33
Sunday. *See* Sabbath

Trinity, the
doctrine of, 27
resurrection of Christ and, 53-
54

Worship. *See* Jesus Christ, worship of